General Lectures On Electrical Engineering

Steinmetz, Charles Proteus, 1865-1923, Hayden, Joseph LeRoy

GENERAL LECTURES

ON

ELECTRICAL ENGINEERING

Mc Graw-Hill Book Co. Inc.

PUBLISHERS OF BOOKS FOR

Coal Age ▽ Electric Railway Journal
Electrical World ▽ Engineering News-Record
American Machinist ▽ The Contractor
Engineering & Mining Journal ▽ Power
Metallurgical & Chemical Engineering
Electrical Merchandising

Charles P. Steinmetz.

GENERAL LECTURES

ON

ELECTRICAL ENGINEERING

BY

CHARLES PROTEUS STEINMETZ, A. M., Ph. D.

FIFTH EDITION

THIRD IMPRESSION

COMPILED AND EDITED BY

JOSEPH LeRoy HAYDEN

McGRAW-HILL BOOK COMPANY, Inc.

NEW YORK. 370 SEVENTH AVENUE

LONDON 6 & 8 BOUVERIE ST, E. C. 4

1918

THE MAPLE PRESS YORK PA

PREFACE TO THE FIFTH EDITION

In the eight years since the earlier editions of "General Lectures on Electrical Engineering" appeared, material changes have taken place in the electrical industry. Electricity has made enormous forward strides, until it now seems destined to become the universal medium of the world's energy, through the agency of huge power generating systems The small electric generating stations and the machinery used in them, are rapidly disappearing before the substations of the unified power system.

The carbon-filament incandescent lamp, after holding sway for a quarter of a century, has become of mere historical interest, and the mazda lamp has taken not only the place of the carbon-filament incandescent lamp, but to a great extent of the arc lamp as well, so that the industrial importance of arc lighting has greatly decreased as compared with that of incandescent lighting

As a result of these and many other developments, the preparation of the fifth edition required material changes and additions to the previous text. A large part of the book has been entirely rewritten, so that as it now stands it differs materially from the previous editions.

Charles Proteus Steinmetz.

Camp Mohawk, Viele's Creek,
   Schenectady, N Y
     September, 1917.

PREFACE TO FIRST EDITION

The following lectures on Electrical Engineering are general in their nature, dealing with the problems of generation, control, transmission, distribution and utilization of electric energy; that is, with the operation of electric systems and apparatus under normal and abnormal conditions, and with the design of such systems, but the design of apparatus is discussed only so far as it is necessary to understand their operation, and so judge of their proper field of application

Due to the nature of the subject, and the limitations of time and space, the treatment had to be essentially descriptive, and not mathematical That is, it comprises a discussion of the different methods of application of electric energy, the means and apparatus available, the different methods of carrying out the purpose, and the relative advantages and disadvantages of the different methods and apparatus, which determine their choice.

It must be realized, however, that such a discussion can be general only, and that there are, and always will be, cases in which, in meeting special conditions, conclusions regarding systems and apparatus may be reached, differing from those which good judgment would dictate under general and average conditions. Thus, for instance, while certain transformer connections are unsafe and should in general be avoided, in special cases it may be found that the danger incidental to their use is so remote as to be overbalanced by some advantages which they may offer in the special case, and their use would thus be justified in this case. That is, in the application of general conclusions to special cases, judgment must be exerted to determine, whether, and how far, they may have to be modified Some such considerations are indicated in the lectures, others must be left to the judgment of the engineer.

The lectures have been collected and carefully edited by my assistant Mr. J. L. R. Hayden, and great thanks are due to the publishers, Messrs. Robson & Adee, for the very creditable and satisfactory form in which they have produced the book. CHARLES P. STEINMETZ.

SCHENECTADY, N Y.
Sept 5, 1908.

CONTENTS

GENERAL LECTURES

ON

ELECTRICAL ENGINEERING

FIRST LECTURE

GENERAL REVIEW

In its economical application, electric power passes through the successive steps; generation, transmission, conversion, distribution and utilization. The requirements regarding the character of the electric power imposed by the successive steps, are generally different, frequently contradictory, and the design of an electric system is therefore a compromise. For instance, electric power can for most purposes be used only at low voltage, 110 to 600 volts, while economical transmission requires the use of as high voltage as possible. For many purposes, as electrolytic work, direct current is necessary, for others, as railroading, preferable; while for transmission, alternating current is preferable, due to the great difficulty of generating and converting high-voltage direct current. In the design of any of the steps through which electric power passes, the requirements of all the other steps so must be taken into consideration. Of the greatest importance in this respect is the use to which electric power is put, since it is the ultimate purpose for which it is generated and transmitted; next in importance is the transmission, as the long-distance transmission line usually is the most expensive part of the system, and in the trans-

1

mission the limitation is more severe than in any other step through which the electric power passes.

The main uses of electric power are:

General distribution for lighting and power. The relative proportion between power use and lighting may vary from the distribution system of many small cities, in which practically all the current is used for lighting, to a power distribution for mills and factories, with only a moderate lighting load in the evening.

The electric railway.

Electrochemistry.

For convenience, the subject will be discussed under the subdivisions:

1. General distribution for lighting and power.
2. Long-distance transmission.
3. Generation.
4. Control and protection.
5. Electric railway.
6. Electrochemistry.
7. Lighting.

CHARACTER OF ELECTRIC POWER

Electric power is used as—

(*a*) Alternating current and direct current.

(*b*) Constant potential and constant current

(*c*) ·High voltage and low voltage.

(*a*) Alternating current is used for transmission, and for general distribution with the exception of the centers of large cities; direct current is usually applied for railroading. For power distribution, both forms of current are used, in electrochemistry, direct current must be used for electrolytic work, while for electric-furnace work alternating current is preferable.

The two standard frequencies of alternating current are 60 cycles and 25 cycles. The former is used for general distribution for lighting and power, the latter is often preferred for conversion to direct current, for alternating-current railways, and for large powers.

In Europe 50 cycles is standard frequency. This frequency still survives in this country in Southern California, where it was introduced before 60 cycles was standard.

The frequencies of 125 to 140 cycles, which were standard in the very early days, 30 years ago, have disappeared.

The frequency of 40 cycles, which once was introduced as compromise between 60 and 25 cycles, is rapidly disappearing, as it is somewhat low for general distribution, and higher than desirable for conversion to direct current. It was largely used also for power distribution in mills and factories as the lowest frequency at which arc and incandescent lighting is still feasible; for the reason that 40-cycle generators driven by slow-speed reciprocating engines are more easily operated in parallel, due to the lower number of poles. With the development of the steam turbine as high-speed prime mover, the conditions in this respect have been reversed, and 60 cycles is more convenient, giving higher turbine speeds. 1800 and 3600 revolutions respectively with the four-polar and bipolar 60-cycle machine, against 750 and 1500 revolutions at 25 cycles, and thereby higher steam economy and lower cost of the turbo-alternator, except in very large sizes.

Sundry odd frequencies, as 30 cycles, 33 cycles, 66 cycles, which were attempted at some points, especially in the early days, have not spread, and frequencies below 25 cycles, as 15 cycles and 8 cycles, as proposed for railroading, have not proved of sufficient advantage so that in general, in the design of an electric system, only the two standard frequencies, 25 and 60 cycles, come into consideration. At present, the tendency is strongly towards 60 cycles, and the use of 60 cycles is extending more rapidly than that of 25 cycles, especially since fairly good 60-cycle converters have been accomplished.

(*b*) Constant current, either alternating or direct, that is, a current of constant amperage, varying in voltage with the load, is mostly used for street lighting by arc lamps and by series incandescent lamps, for all other purposes, constant potential is employed.

(*c*) For long-distance transmission, the highest permissible voltage is used; for primary distribution by alternating current, 2200 volts, that is, voltages between 2000 and 2600; for alternating-current secondary distribution, and direct-current distribution, 220 to 260 volts and occasionally twice this voltage, and for direct-current railroading, 550 to 600 volts, and occasionally 1200, 1800 and even 2400 and 5000 volts, for alternating-current railroading usually 11,000 volts

1. General Distribution for Lighting and Power.— In general distribution for lighting and power, direct current and 60 cycles alternating current are available   Twenty-five cycles alternating current is not well suited, since it does not permit arc lighting, and for incandescent lighting it is just at the limit, where under some conditions and with some generator waves, flickering shows, while with others it does not show appreciably.

The distribution voltage is determined by the limitation of the incandescent lamp, or about 110 volts.   One hundred and ten volts is too low to distribute with good regulation, that is, with negligible voltage drop, any appreciable amount of power, and so practically always twice that voltage is employed in the distribution, by using a three-wire system, with 110 volts between outside and neutral, and 220 volts between the outside conductors, as shown diagrammatically in Fig. 1. By approximately balancing the load between the two circuits, the current in the neutral conductor is very small, the drop of voltage so negligible, and the distribution, regarding voltage drop and copper economy, so takes place at 220 volts, while the lamps operate at 110 volts. Even where a separate transformer feeds a single house, usually a three-wire distribution is preferable, if the number of lamps is not very small.

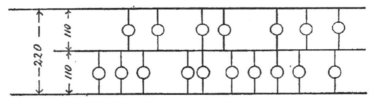

FIG. 1.—Typical three-wire lighting circuit.

Two hundred and twenty-volt distribution, with 440 volts between the outside conductors, has been tried but found uneconomical in this country, due to the lower efficiency of the 220-volt lamp.

In this country, 110-volt lamps are therefore used almost exclusively, while in England, for instance, 220-volt lamps are largely used, in a three-wire distribution system with 440 volts between the outside conductors. The amount of copper required in the distribution system, with the same loss of power in the distributing conductors, is inversely proportional to the square of the voltage. That is, at twice the voltage, twice the voltage drop can be allowed for the same distribution efficiency; and as at double voltage the current is one-half, for the same load

twice the voltage drop at half the current gives four times
the resistance, that is, one-quarter the conductor material.
By the change from the 220-volt distribution with 110-
volt lamps, to the 440-volt distribution with 220-volt
lamps, the amount of copper in the distributing conductor,
and thereby the cost of investment can be greatly reduced,
and current supplied over greater distances, so that from
the point of view of the economical supply of current at
the customers' terminals, the higher voltage is preferable
However, in the usual sizes, from 50 to 60 watts power consumption and so 16 candlepower with the old carbon
filament, and to a much larger extent still with the metal-
filament lamp, as the tungsten lamp, the 220-volt lamp
is materially less efficient, that is, requires from 10 to 15
per cent more power than the 110-volt lamp, when producing the same amount of light at the same useful life.
This difference is inherent in the incandescent lamp, and
is due to the far greater length and smaller section of the
220-volt filament, compared with the 110-volt filament,
and therefore no possibility of overcoming it exists; if it
should be possible to build a 220-volt lamp as efficient—
at the same useful life—as the present 110- volt lamp, this
would simply mean, that by the same improvement the
efficiency of the 110-volt lamp could also be increased from
10 to 15 per cent , and the difference would remain.   For
small units, the difference in efficiency is still greater.

Indeed, in England and those countries where 220-
volt distribution is extensively used, the introduction of
the tungsten lamp—commonly called "mazda lamp"—
has been, and still is very seriously retarded, to the great
disadvantage of the user of the light.

The loss of efficiency of 10 to 15 per cent., resulting
from the use of the 220-volt lamp, is far greater than the

saving in power and in cost of investment in the supply mains, and the 220-volt system with 110-volt lamps is therefore more efficient, in the amount of light produced in the customer's lamps, than the 440-volt system with 220-volt lamps In this country, since the early days, the illuminating companies have accepted the responsibility up to the output in light at the customer's lamps, by supplying and renewing the lamps free of charge, and the system using 110-volt lamps is therefore universally employed while the 220-volt lamp has no right to existence; while abroad, where the supply company considers its responsibility ended at the customer's meter, and the customer is left to supply his own lamps, the supply company saves by the use of 440-volt systems—at the expense of a waste of power in the customer's 220-volt lamps, far more than the saving effected by the supply company

The general use of 110-volt distribution in this country, and the extended use of 220 volts abroad, thus is the result of a difference in the policy of the lighting companies, more particular the large Edison companies, which under the inspiration of Edison took the responsibility of giving the customer the maximum light producible at a given cost, by not only supplying the power, but also the lamps. The policy of free lamp renewals thus has been the most important cause which has brought about and maintained the superiority of the lighting service of the American supply companies. With the introduction of the metal-filament lamp, with its higher cost and lesser power consumption, for some years this policy of free lamp renewals, on which the American superiority is based, was seriously threatened; but it is fortunate that by cooperation of lamp manufacturer and supply company the prices of tungsten lamps have been sufficiently lowered, and their life increased, so as to make it possible to return to free lamp renewals with the mazda lamp, and thereby safeguard the quality and efficiency of the lamps used by the customers, and with it the superior quality of the lighting service

When speaking of a distribution voltage of 110, some voltage anywhere in the range from 105 to 130 volts is meant, and the various distribution systems of our country have chosen various voltages within this wide range, to secure best economy of the incandescent lamp   In the manufacture of the carbon-filament lamp of old, only two of the three quantities efficiency, wattage and voltage, could be made exact according to specifications.   Thus in treating the lamp, its voltage could be made right at the desired wattage—but then the efficiency might be a little off—or the desired efficiency could be produced at the desired wattage—but the voltage might be a little different from specifications.   Thus either a relatively wide margin would have to be allowed in complying with the specifications, that is, a fairly irregular product accepted, or a considerable percentage of the lamps would not meet specifications, resulting in increased cost.   This difficulty was met by producing the lamps exact regarding efficiency and wattage, and then assorting them by voltage, and by agreement between lamp manufacturer and lighting companies, various operating voltages were chosen by the latter, so as to utilize the entire lamp product   Hereby a very close rating of the lamps, and correspondingly high uniformity and economy of the lighting systems were secured, but this feature led to the large number of distribution voltages.

However, the carbon-filament lamp has now practically disappeared, and in the mazda lamp, the tungsten wire, drawn to exact diameter and cut off to exact length, fixed definitely the efficiency, wattage and voltage, so that the need of the many distribution voltages has disappeared, and they are rather a serious economic disadvantage, by requiring numerous lamp voltage standards. Therefore, a strong movement exists to reduce the distribution voltages again to the least possible number, perhaps three or four, and correspondingly reduce the number of lamp standards, and as this is in the direction of increased economy, it will undoubtedly be brought about, though it will probably not be possible to go to one single standard lamp voltage only. However, sometimes more than one standard voltage may be desirable, as in an extended distribution system a higher lamp voltage may be chosen as standard near the substation, than at a distance, and the problem of voltage regulation thereby somewhat simplified.

In considering distribution systems, it therefore is unnecessary to consider any other lamp voltage than 110 volts (that is, the range of voltage represented thereby).

In direct-current distribution systems, as used in most large cities, the 220-volt network is fed from a direct-current generating station, or—as now more frequently is the case—from a converter substation, which receives its power as three-phase alternating, from the main generating station, or long-distance transmission line. In alternating-current distribution, the 220-volt distribution circuits are fed by step-down transformers from the 2200-volt primary distribution system. In the latter case, where considerable motor load has to be considered, some arrangement of polyphase supply is desirable, as the single-phase motor is inferior to the polyphase motor, and so the latter is preferable for large and moderate sizes.

COMPARISON OF ALTERNATING CURRENT AND DIRECT CURRENT

At the low distribution voltage of 220, current can economically be supplied from a moderate distance only, rarely exceeding from 1 to 2 miles. In a direct-current system, the current must be supplied from a generating station or a converter substation, that is, a station containing revolving machinery. As such a station requires continuous attention, its operation would hardly be economical if not of a capacity of at least some hundred kilowatts. The direct-current distribution system therefore can be used economically only if a sufficient demand exists, within a radius of 1 to 2 miles, to load a good-sized generator or converter substation. The use of direct current is therefore restricted to those places where a fairly concentrated load exists, as in large cities, while in the suburbs, and in small cities and villages, where the load is too scattered to reach, from one low-tension supply point, sufficient customers to load a substation, the alternating current must be used, as it requires merely a step-down transformer which needs no attention,

However, in the last years, some automatic converter substations have been developed, which operate very satisfactorily without any attendance beyond an occasional inspection.

In the interior of large cities, the alternating-current system is at a disadvantage, because in addition to the voltage consumed by resistance, an additional drop of voltage occurs by self-induction, or by reactance; and with the large conductors required for the distribution of a large low-tension current, the drop of voltage by self-induction is far greater than that by resistance, and the regulation of the system therefore is seriously impaired, or at least the voltage regulation becomes far more difficult than with direct current. A second disadvantage of the alternating current for distribution in large cities is, that a considerable part of the motor load is elevator motors, and the alternating-current elevator motor is still somewhat inferior to the direct-current motor Elevator service essentially consists in starting at heavy torque, and rapid acceleration, and in both of these features the direct-current motor with compound field winding is superior, and easier to control.

Where therefore direct current can be used in low-tension distribution, it is preferable to use it, and to relegate alternating-current low-tension distribution to those cases where direct current cannot be used, that is, where the load is not sufficiently concentrated to economically operate converter substations.

The loss of power in the low-tension direct-current system is merely the i^2r loss in the conductors, which is zero at no load, and increases with the load; the only constant loss in a direct-current distribution system is the loss of power in the shunt coils of the integrating wattmeters on the customer's premises. In the direct-current system, therefore, the efficiency of distribution is highest at light load, and decreases with increasing load.

In an alternating-current distribution system, with a 2200-volt primary distribution, feeding secondary low-tension circuits by step-down transformers, the i^2r loss in the conductors usually is far smaller than in the direct-current system, but a considerable constant, or "no-load," loss exists; the core loss in the transformers, and the efficiency of an alternating-current distribution is usually lowest at light load, but increases with increase of load, since with increasing load the transformer core loss becomes a lesser and lesser percentage of the total power. The i^2r loss in alternating-current systems must be far lower than in direct-current systems:

1. Because it is not the only loss, and the existence of the "no-load" or transformer core loss requires to reduce the load loss or i^2r loss, if an equally good efficiency is desired. With an alternating-current system, each low-tension main requires only a step-down transformer, which needs no attention, therefore, many more transformers can be used than rotary converter substations in a direct-current system, and the i^2r loss is then reduced by the greatly reduced distance of secondary distribution.

2. In the alternating-current system, the drop of voltage in the conductors is greater than the ir drop by the self-inductive drop; the ir drop is therefore only a part of the total voltage drop; and with the same voltage drop and therefore the same regulation as a direct-current system, the i^2r loss in the alternating-current system would be smaller than in the direct-current system.

3 Due to the self-inductive drop, smaller and, therefore, more numerous low-tension distribution circuits must be used with alternating current than with direct current, and a separate and independent voltage regulation of each low-tension circuit—that is—each transformer, therefore, usually becomes impracticable. This means that the total voltage drop, resistance and inductance, in the alternating-current low-tension distribution circuits must be kept within a few per cent., that is, within the range permissible by the incandescent lamp. As a result thereof, the voltage regulation of an alternating-current low-tension distribution has frequently been inferior to that of the direct-current distribution—in many cases to such

an extent as to require the use of incandescent lamps of lower efficiency.

However, by the extended use of voltage regulators in the primary alternating-current feeders, good voltage regulation is secured in the better class of alternating-current distribution systems.

SECOND LECTURE

GENERAL DISTRIBUTION

DIRECT-CURRENT DISTRIBUTION

The typical direct-current distribution is the system of feeders and mains, as devised by Edison, and since used in all direct-current distributions. It is shown diagrammatically in Fig 2 The conductors are usually underground, as direct-current systems are used only in large cities. A system of three-wire conductors, called the "mains" is laid in the streets of the city, shown diagrammatically by the heavily drawn lines Commonly, conductors of 1,000,000 circular mil section (that is, a copper section which as solid round conductor would have a diameter of 1″) are used for the outside conductors, the "positive" and the "negative" conductor; and a conductor of half this size for the middle or "neutral" conductor. The latter is usually grounded, as protection against fire risk, etc. Conductors of more than 1,000,000 circular mils are generally not used, but when the load exceeds the capacity of such conductors, a second main is laid in the same street. A number of feeders, shown by dotted lines in Fig. 2, radiate from the generating station or converter substations, and tap into the mains at numerous points; potential wires run back from the mains to the station, and so allow of measuring, in the station, the voltage at the different points of the distribution system. All the customers are connected to the mains, but none to the feeders. The mains and feeders are

14

arranged so that no appreciable voltage drop takes place
in the mains, but all drop of voltage occurs in the feeders;
and as no customers connect to the feeders, the only

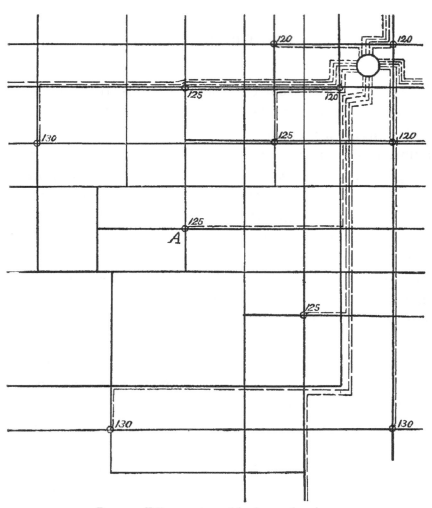

FIG. 2.—Edison system of feeders and mains.

limit to the voltage drop in the feeders is efficiency of
distribution. The voltage at the feeding points into the
mains is kept constant by varying the voltage supply
to the feeders with the changes of the load on the mains.

This is done by having a number of outside busbars in the station, as shown diagrammatically in Fig. 3, differing from each other in voltage, and connecting feeders over from busbar to busbar, with the change of load.

For instance, in a 2 × 120 voltage distribution, the station may have, in addition to the neutral busbar zero, three positive busbars 1, 1', 1'', and three negative busbars 2, 2', 2'', differing respectively from the neutral bus by 120, 125 and 130 volts, as shown in Fig. 3. At light load, when the drop of voltage in the feeders is negligible, the

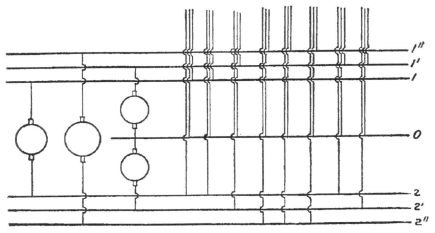

FIG. 3.—Three-wire direct-current station.

feeders connect to the buses 1, 0, 2 of 120 volts. When the load increases, some of the feeders are shifted over, by transfer busbars, to the 125-volt busbars 1' and 2'; with still further increase of load, more feeders are connected over to 125 volts; then some feeders are connected to the 130-volt busbars, 1'' and 2'', and so, by varying the voltage supply to the feeders, the voltage at the mains can be maintained constant with an accuracy depending on the number of busbars. It is obvious that a shift of a feeder from one voltage to another does not mean a corresponding voltage change on the main supplied by it, but rather a shift of load between the feeders, and so a readjustment of the total voltage in the territory near the supply point of the feeder. For instance, if by the potential wires a drop of voltage below 120 volts is registered in the main at the connection point of feeder A in Fig 2, and this feeder then shifted from the supply voltage 125 to 130, the current in the main near A, which before flowed toward A as minimum voltage point, reverses in direction, flows away from A, the load on feeder A increases, and, therefore, the drop of voltage in A increases, while the load on the adjacent feeders decreases, and thereby their drop of voltage decreases, with the result of bringing up the voltage in the mains at the feeder A and all adjacent feeders   This interlinkage of feeders, therefore, allows a regulation of voltage in the mains, far closer than the number of voltages available in the station

Originally, such direct-current Edison distribution systems were fed from a number of direct-current generating stations, having machine units—generally direct-connected to slow-speed steam engines—each consisting of two 125-volt generators, connected respectively between the neutral and the two outside conductors of the system. Such direct-current generating systems have entirely disappeared, and been replaced by substations fed with power from one or a number of high-power high-voltage three-phase alternating power-generating stations (except in local isolated plants, such as sometimes used in office buildings, hotels, etc.).

In the substation, three-wire synchronous converters are most frequently used, that is, 250-volt converters in which the neutral is brought out by collector rings and derived by auto-transformer.   Sometimes the neutral

2

is derived by a separate balancer set, a pair of 125-volt machines connected in series between the three lines, or from the storage battery; induction or synchronous motor-driven direct-current generators are also occasionally used, especially where the alternating supply is of 60 cycles, and sometimes two separate 125-volt generators or converters in series, though the latter arrangement has practically gone out of use, by its inefficiency.

The different busbars in the station are supplied with their voltage by having different generators or converters in the station operate at different voltages, and with increasing load on the station, and consequent increasing demand of higher voltage by the feeders, shift machines from lower to higher-voltage busbars, inversely with decreasing load, or the different busbars are operated through boosters, or by connection with the storage-battery reserve, etc.

In addition to feeders and mains, tie feeders usually connect the generating station or substation with adjacent stations, so that during periods of light load, or in case of breakdown, a station may be shut down altogether and supplied from adjacent stations by tie feeders. Such tie feeders also permit most stations to operate without storage-battery reserve, that is, to concentrate the storage batteries in a few stations, from which in case of a breakdown of the system, the other stations are supplied over the tie feeders

All more important direct-current distribution systems contain a storage-battery reserve, capable of maintaining service in case of complete accident and shutdown, until the machinery can be started up again.

ALTERNATING-CURRENT DISTRIBUTION

The system of feeders and mains allows the most perfect voltage regulation in the distributing mains. It is, however, applicable only to direct-current distribution in a territory of very concentrated load, as in the interior of a large city, since the independent voltage regulation of each one of numerous feeders is economically permissible only where each feeder represents a large amount of power; with alternating-current systems, the inductive drop forbids the concentration of such large currents in a single conductor. That is, conductors of 1,000,000 circular mils cannot be used economically in an alternating-current system.

The resistance of a conductor is inversely proportional to the size or section of the conductor, hence decreases rapidly with increasing current a conductor of 1,000,000 circular mils is one-tenth the resistance of a conductor of 100,000 circular mils, and so can carry ten times the direct current with the same voltage drop The reactance of a conductor, however, and so the voltage consumed by self-induction, decreases only very little with the increasing size of a conductor, as seen from the table of resistances and reactances of conductors given in Appendix II. A wire No. 000 B. & S. gage is eight times the section of a wire No. 7, and, therefore, one-eighth the resistance; but the wire No 000 has a reactance of 0.109 ohm per 1000 feet, the wire No. 7 has a reactance of 0.133 ohm, or only 1 22 times as large Hence, while in the wire No 7, the reactance, at 60 cycles, is only 0.266 times the resistance and, therefore, not of serious importance, in a wire No 000 the reactance is 1.76 times the resistance, and the latter conductor is likely to give a voltage drop far in excess of the ohmic resistance drop. The ratio of reactance to resistance, therefore, rapidly increases with increasing size of conductor, and for alternating currents, large conductors cannot, therefore, be used economically where close voltage regulation is required.

With alternating currents it, therefore, is preferable to use several smaller conductors in multiple. two conductors of No 1 in multiple have the same resistance as one conductor of No. 000, but the reactance of one conductor No. 000 is 0.109 ohm, and so 1 88 times as great as the reactance of two conductors of No. 1 in multiple, which latter is half that of one conductor No. 1, or 0.058 ohm, provided that the two conductors are used as separate circuits.

In alternating-current low-tension distribution, the size of the conductor and so the current per conductor, is limited by the self-inductive drop, and alternating-current low-tension networks are, therefore, of necessity of smaller size than those of direct-current distribution

As regards economy of distribution, this is not a serious objection, as the alternating-current transformer and primary distribution permits the use of numerous secondary circuits.

In alternating-current systems, a primary distribution system of 2200 volts is used, feeding step-down transformers.

The different arrangements are—

(a) A separate transformer for each customer. This is necessary in those cases where the customers are so far apart from each other that they cannot be reached by the same low tension or secondary circuit; every alternating-current system, therefore, has at least a number of instances where individual transformers are used.

This is the most uneconomical arrangement. It requires the use of small transformers, which are necessarily less efficient and more expensive per kilowatt, than large transformers The transformer must be built to carry, within its overload capacity, all the lamps installed by the

customer, since all the lamps may be used occasionally
Usually, however, only a small part of the lamps are in
use, and those only for a small part of the day; so that the
average load on the transformer is a very small part of its
capacity. As the core loss in the transformer continues
whether the transformer is loaded or not, but is not paid
for by the customer, the economy of the arrangement is
very low, and so it can be understood that in the early
days, where this arrangement was generally used, the
financial results of most alternating-current distributions
were very discouraging

Assuming as an instance a connected load of 20 : 60 watt
lamps, allowing then in cases of all lamps being used, an
overload of 100 per cent , which is rather beyond safe limits,
and permissible only on the assumption that this load will
occur very rarely, and for a short time –the transformer
would have 600-watt rating. Assuming a core loss of 4 per
cent., this gives a continuous power consumption of 24 watts.
Usually probably only one or two lamps will be burning,
and these only a few hours per day, so that the use of two
lamps, at an average—summer and winter—of 3 hours per
day, would probably be a fair example of many such
cases. Two lamps or 120 watts, for 3 hours per day, give
an average power of 15 watts. which is paid for by the
customer, while the continuous loss in the transformer is
24 watts; so that the all-year efficiency, or the ratio of the
power paid for by the customer, to the power consumed
by the transformer, is only $\frac{15}{15 + 24}$ or 38 per cent.

By connecting several adjacent customers to the same
transformer, the conditions immediately become far more
favorable It is extremely improbable that all the customers will burn all their lamps at the same time, the

more so, the greater the number of customers is, which are supplied from the same transformer It, therefore, becomes unnecessary to allow a transformer capacity capable of operating all the connected load. The larger transformer also has a higher efficiency. Assuming, therefore, as an instance, four customers of 20 lamps connected load each. The average load would be about 8 lamps Assuming even one customer burning all 20 lamps, it is not probable that the other customers together would at this time burn more than 10 to 15 lamps, and a transformer carrying 30 to 35 lamps at overload would probably be sufficient. A 1500-watt transformer would therefore be larger than necessary. At 3 per cent core loss, this gives a constant loss of 45 watts, while an average load of 8 lamps for 3 hours per day gives a useful output of 60 watts, or an all-year efficiency of nearly 60 per cent., while a 1000-watt transformer would give an all-year efficiency of 67 per cent.

This also illustrates that in smaller transformers a low core loss is of utmost importance, while the i^2r loss is of very much less importance, since it is appreciable only at heavy load, and, therefore, affects the all-year efficiency very little

When it becomes possible to connect a large number of customers to a secondary main fed from one large transformer the connected load ceases to be of moment in the transformer capacity; the transformer capacity is determined by the average load, with a safe margin for overloads; in this case, good all-year efficiencies can be reached, as the average load rarely exceeds one-third of the connected load.

Economical alternating-current distribution, therefore, requires the use of secondary distribution mains of as large an extent as possible, fed by large transformers. The distance, however, to which a transformer can supply secondary current, is rather limited by the inductive drop of voltage; therefore, for supplying secondary mains, transformers of larger size than 60 kilowatts are rarely used, but rather several transformers are employed, to feed in the same main at different points.

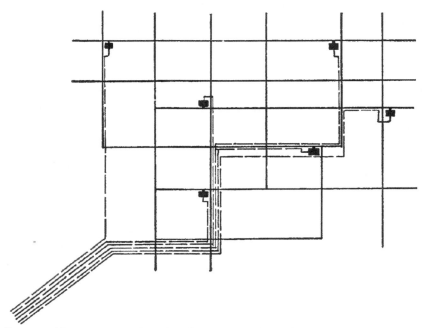

Fig. 4.—Alternating current distribution with secondary mains and primary feeders.

Extending the secondary mains still further by the use of several transformers feeding into the same mains, or, as it may be considered, interconnecting the secondary mains of the different transformers, we arrive at a system somewhat similar to the direct-current system: a low-tension distribution system of 220 volts three-wire mains, with a system of feeders tapping into it at a number of points, as shown in Fig. 4. These feeders are primary feeders of

2200 volts, connecting to the mains through step-down transformers. In such a system, by varying the voltage impressed upon the primary feeders, a voltage regulation of the system similar to that of direct-current distribution becomes feasible. Such an arrangement has the advantages over the direct-current system, that the drop in the feeders is very much lower, due to their higher voltage, and the feeder voltage can be regulated by alternating-current feeder regulators or auto-transformers, that is, stationary structures similar to the transformer. It has, however, the disadvantage that, due to the self-induction of the mains, each feeding point can supply current over a far shorter distance than with direct current, and the interchange of current between feeders, by which the load can be shifted and apportioned between the feeders, is far less.

As a result, it is difficult to reach as good voltage regulation with the same attention to the system; and since this arrangement has the disadvantage that any breakdown in the secondary system or in a transformer may involve the entire system, this system of interconnected secondary mains is rarely used for alternating-current distribution, but the secondary mains are usually kept separate. That is, as shown diagrammatically in Fig 5, a number of separate secondary mains are fed by large transformers from primary feeders, and usually each primary feeder connects to a number of transformers. Where the distances are considerable, and the voltage drop in the primary feeders appreciable, voltage regulation of the feeders becomes necessary; and in this case, to get good voltage regulation in the system, attention must be given to the arrangements of the feeders and mains. That is, all the transformers on the same feeder should be at about the same distance from the station, so that the voltage drop between the transformers on the same feeder is negligible; and the nature of the load on the secondary

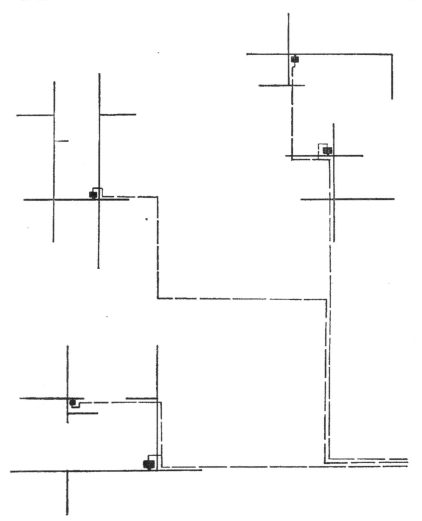

FIG. 5.—Typical alternating-current distribution.

mains fed by the same feeder should be about as nearly the same as feasible, so that all the mains on the same feeder are about equally loaded.   It may, therefore, be undesirable for voltage regulation, to connect, for instance, a main feeding a residential section to the same feeder as a main feeding a business district or an office building.

In a well-designed alternating-current distribution system, that is, a system using secondary distribution mains as far as feasible, the all-year efficiency is about the same as with the direct-current system. In such an alternating-current system, the efficiency at heavy load is higher, and at light load lower, than in the direct-current system; in this respect the alternating-current system has the advantage over the direct-current system, since at the time of heavy load the power is more valuable than at light load.

THIRD LECTURE

LIGHT AND POWER DISTRIBUTION

In a direct-current distribution system, the motor load is connected to the outside mains at 220 volts, and only very small motors, as fan motors, between outside mains and neutral; since the latter connection, with a large motor, would locally unbalance a system The effect of a motor on the system depends upon its size and starting current, and with the large mains and feeders, which are generally used, even the starting of large elevator motors has no appreciable effect, and the supply of power to electric elevators represents a very important use of direct-current distribution

In alternating-current distribution systems, the effect on the voltage regulation, when starting a motor, is more severe, since alternating-current motors in starting usually take a larger current than direct-current motors starting with the same torque on the same voltage, and the current of the alternating-current motor is lagging, the voltage drop caused by it in the reactance is, therefore, greater than would be caused by the same current taken by a non-inductive load, as lamps. Furthermore, alternating-current supply mains usually are of far smaller capacity, and, therefore, more affected in voltage Large motors are, therefore, rarely connected to the lighting mains of an alternating-current system, but separate transformers and frequently separate feeders are used for the motors, and very large motors are commonly built for the primary distribution voltage of 2200, and connected to these mains.

27

For use in an alternating-current distribution system, the synchronous motor hardly comes into consideration, since the synchronous type is suitable mainly for large powers, where it is operated on a separate circuit

The alternating-current motor mostly used in small and moderate sizes—such as come into consideration for power distribution from a general supply system—is the induction motor and, where high torque starting and acceleration or adjustable speed are desirable, the repulsion-induction motor, which is a single-phase alternating commutator motor The single-phase induction motor, however, is so inferior to the polyphase induction motor, that single-phase motors are used only in small sizes, for medium and larger sizes the three-phase or two-phase motor is preferred or a commutator motor is used. The former, however, introduces a complication in the distribution system, and the three-wire single-phase system, therefore, is less suited for motor supply, but additional conductors have to be added to give a polyphase power supply to the motor. As the result thereof, motors are not used in alternating-current systems to the same extent as in direct-current systems. In the alternating-current system, however, the motor load is, if anything, more important than in the direct-current system, to increase the load factor of the system; since the efficiency of the ·alternating-current system decreases with decrease of load, while that of a direct-current system increases.

Compared with the direct-current motor, the polyphase induction motor has the disadvantage of being less flexible: its speed cannot be varied economically, as that of a direct-current motor by varying the field excitation Speed variation of the induction motor produced by a rheostat in the armature or secondary circuit is accomplished by wasting power the power input of an induction motor always corresponds to full speed; if the speed is reduced by running on the rheostat, the difference in power between that which the motor actually gives, and that which it would give, with the same torque, at full speed, is consumed in the rheostat.

Where, therefore, different motor speeds are required, provisions are made in the induction motor to change the number of poles; thereby a number of different definite speeds are available, at which the motor operates economically as "multispeed" motor.

The starting torque of the polyphase induction motor with starting rheostat in the armature is the same as the running torque at the same current input, just as in the case of the direct-current shunt motor with constant field excitation. In the squirrel-cage induction motor, however, the starting torque is far less than the running torque at the same current input; or inversely, to produce the same starting torque, a greater starting current is required. In starting torque or current, the squirrel-cage induction motor has the disadvantage against the direct-current motor. It has, however, an enormous advantage over it in its greater simplicity and reliability, due to the absence of commutator and brushes, and the use of a squirrel-cage armature.

The advantage of simplicity and reliability of the squirrel-cage induction motor sufficiently compensates for the disadvantage of the large starting current, to make the motor most commonly used. In an alternating-current distribution system, however, great care has to be taken to avoid the use of such larger motors at places where their heavy lagging starting currents may affect the voltage regulation, in such places, separate transformers and even separate primary feeders are desirable.

The single-phase induction motor is not desirable in larger sizes in a distribution system, since its starting current is still larger, in small sizes, however, it is extensively used, since it requires no special conductors, but can be operated from a single-phase lighting main.

The alternating-current commutator motor is a single-phase motor which has all the advantages of the different types of direct-current motors; it can be built as constant-speed motor of the shunt type, or as motor with the characteristics of the direct-current series motor: very high starting torque with moderate starting current It has, however, also the disadvantages of the direct-current motor: commutator and brushes, and so requires more attention than the squirrel-cage induction motor

However, this disadvantage usually is not very serious, and the advantages of such alternating-current commutator motors to operate on single-phase distribution circuits, to give high starting torque efficiency, that is, start under load with moderate current, to allow efficient speed variation by what in its principle amounts to field control, and the possibility of giving very high power factors, has led to the development and extensive introduction of such single-phase commutator motors, usually of the type of the repulsion motor or the compensated repulsion motor.

Alternating-current generators now are almost always used as three-phase machines, and transmission lines are always three-phase, though in transforming down, the system can be changed to two-phase. The power supply in an alternating-current system, therefore, is practically always polyphase; and since a motor load, which is very desirable for economical operation, also requires polyphase currents, alternating-current distribution systems always start from polyphase power

The problem of alternating-current distribution, therefore, is to supply, from a polyphase generating system, single-phase current to the incandescent lamps, and polyphase current to the induction motors.

PRIMARY DISTRIBUTION SYSTEMS

1. Two conductors of the three-phase generating or transmission system are used to supply a 2200 single-phase system for lighting by step-down transformers and three-wire secondary mains, the third conductor is carried to those places where motors are used and three-phase motors are operated by separate step-down transformers. In the lighting feeders, the voltage is then controlled by feeder regulators, or, in a smaller system, the generator excitation is varied so as to maintain the proper voltage on the lighting phase At load, the three-phase triangle then more or less unbalances, but induction motors are very little sensitive to unbalancing of the voltage, and by their regulation—by taking more current from the phase of higher, less from the phase of lower voltage—tend to restore the balance. For smaller motors, frequently two transformers are used, arranged in "open delta" connection

2. Two-phase generators are used, or in the step-down transformers of a three-phase transmission line, the voltage is changed from three-phase to two-phase; the lighting feeders are distributed between the two phases and controlled by potential regulators so that the distribution for lighting is single-phase, by three-wire secondary mains. For motors, both phases are brought together, and the voltage stepped down for use on two-phase motors. This

requires four, or at least three, primary wires to motor loads. This system is only rarely used today.

3. From three-phase generators or transmission lines, three separate single-phase systems are operated for lighting, that is the lighting feeders with their voltage regulators are distributed between the three phases, and all three primary wires are brought to the step-down transformers for motors. This arrangement, by distributing the lighting feeders between the three phases, would require more care in exactly balancing the load between all three phases than two, but a much greater unbalancing can be allowed without affecting the voltage. Separate feeder regulators then are used in the three phases.

4. Four-wire three-phase primary distribution with neutral wire, which sometimes is grounded, and 2200 volts between outside conductors and neutral. The lighting feeders are distributed between the three circuits between outside conductors and neutral, and motors supplied by three of such transformers. This system is now very frequently used, and is becoming of increasing importance, since it allows economical distribution to distances beyond those which can be reached with 2200 volts: with 2600 volts on the transformers—as the upper limit of primary distribution voltage—the voltage between outside conductors is 4500, and the copper economy of the system, therefore, is that of a 4500-volt three-phase system.

5. Polyphase primary and polyphase secondary distribution, with the motors connected to the same secondary mains as the lights. This system is largely used only where most of the load is power distribution, as in factories, etc.

6. Six thousand six hundred volts and 13,200 volts single-phase and three-phase are increasingly being used

in primary distribution in less densely populated territories and with power derived from a very high-voltage transmission line, especially in the West.

In supplying villages and other small settlements with electric power from a very high-voltage transmission line, 100,000 volts for instance, the difficulty is that transformation from such high voltages becomes economical only in larger units, hundreds of kilowatts, and the power demand of a village or smaller settlement is rarely as large as this, thus can be economically met only by choosing a primary distribution voltage sufficiently high to supply a number of places from the same step-down transformer. Six thousand six hundred volts and in less densely populated districts 13,200 volts have been found well suited for this purpose.

SYSTEMS OF LOW-TENSION DISTRIBUTION FOR LIGHTING AND POWER

1. Two-wire, Direct-current or Single-phase, 110 Volts (Fig. 6).—This can be used only for very short distances,

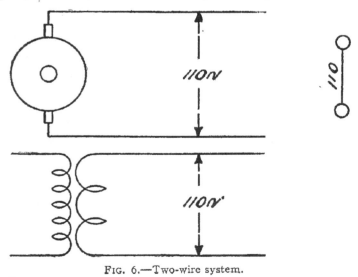

FIG. 6.—Two-wire system.

3

since its copper economy is very low, that is, the amount of conductor material is very high for a given power.

In comparing the copper efficiency of different systems this usually is considered as unity, that is: Cu 1

2. Three-wire, Direct-current or Single-phase, 110 to 220 Volts (Fig. 7).—Neutral one-half size of the two outside

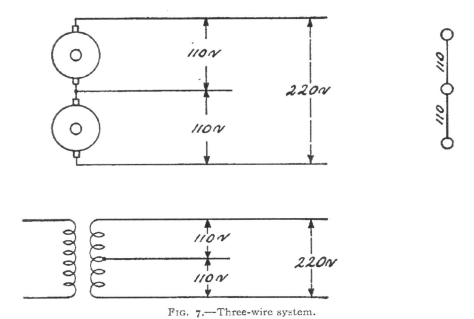

Fig. 7.—Three-wire system.

conductors. The two outside conductors require one-quarter the copper of the two wires of a 110-volt system; since at twice the voltage and one-half the current, four times the resistance or one-quarter the copper is sufficient for the same loss (the amount of conductor material varying with the square of the voltage).

Adding then one-quarter for the neutral of half-size, gives $\frac{1}{4} \times \frac{1}{4} = \frac{1}{16}$ or altogether $\frac{1}{4} + \frac{1}{16} = \frac{5}{16}$ of the conductor material required by the two-wire 110-volt system.

That is, the copper economy is $\frac{5}{16}$. This is the most commonly used system, since it is very economical, and requires only three conductors. It is, however, a single-phase system, and, therefore, not suitable for operating polyphase induction motors. Cu $\frac{5}{16}$

3. Four-wire Quarter-phase (Two-phase) (Fig. 8).—
Two separate two-wire single-phase circuits, therefore, no

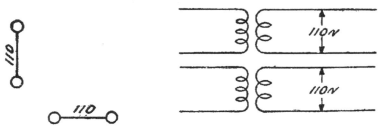

FIG. 8—Four-wire two-phase system.

saving in copper over two-wire systems. That is, the copper economy is: Cu 1

This system is only little used.

4. Three-wire Quarter-phase (Fig. 9).—Common return of both phases, therefore, saves one wire or one-quarter of the copper; hence has the copper economy: Cu $\frac{3}{4}$

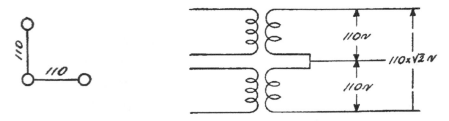

FIG. 9.—Three-wire two-phase system.

In this case, however, the middle or common return wire carries $\sqrt{2}$, or 1.41 times as much current as the other two wires, and when making all three wires of the same size, the copper is not used most economically. A small further saving is, therefore, made by increasing the middle wire and decreasing the outside wires so that the middle wire has 1.41 times the section of each outside wire. This improves the copper economy to: Cu 0.73

This system is used in special cases only.

5. Three-wire Three-phase (Fig. 10).—A three-phase system is best considered as a combination of three single-phase systems, of the voltage from line to neutral, and with zero return (because the three currents neutralize each other in the neutral).

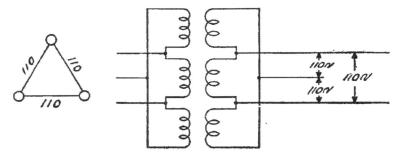

Fig. 10.—Three-wire three-phase system.

Compared thereto the two-wire single-phase system can be considered as a combination of two single-phase circuits from wire to neutral with zero return.

In a 110-volt single-phase system the voltage from line to neutral equals $110 \frac{1}{2}$, in a three-phase system equals $\frac{110}{\sqrt{3}}$.

The ratio of voltages is $\frac{110}{2} \div \frac{110}{\sqrt{3}}$, or $\frac{110 \times \sqrt{3}}{2 \times 110} = \sqrt{3/4}$ and the square of the ratio of voltages equals $3/4$; and as the copper economy varies with the square of the voltage, the copper economy for the three-wire three-phase system is:

Cu $3/4$

This system is going out of use.

6. Five-wire Quarter-phase (Fig. 11).—Neglecting the neutral conductor, the five-wire quarter-phase system can be considered as four single-phase circuits without return, from line to neutral, of voltage 110. Compared with the two-wire circuit, which consists of two single-phase circuits

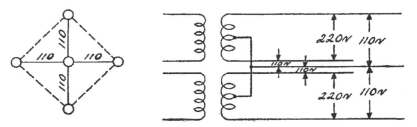

FIG. 11.—Five-wire two-phase system.

without return, of $110\frac{1}{2}$ volts, No. 6, therefore, has twice the voltage of No. 1; therefore, one-quarter the copper.

Making the neutral half the size of the main conductor adds one-half of the copper of one conductor, or $\frac{1}{8}$ of $\frac{1}{4}$ = $\frac{1}{32}$, so giving a total of $\frac{1}{4} + \frac{1}{32}$, that is, a copper economy of: $\qquad$ Cu $\frac{9}{32}$

Due to the large number of conductors required, this system is rarely used.

7. Four-wire Three-phase (Fig. 12).—Lamps connected between line and neutral.

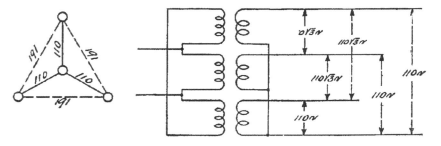

FIG. 12.—Four-wire three-phase system.

Neglecting the neutral, the system consists of three single-phase circuits without return, of 110 volts, and compared with the two-wire circuit of $110\frac{1}{2}$ between wire and neutral without return, it, therefore, requires one-quarter the copper.

Making the neutral one-half size adds $\frac{1}{6}$ of the copper, or $\frac{1}{6}$ of $\frac{1}{4} = \frac{1}{24}$, and so gives a total copper economy of $\frac{1}{24} + \frac{1}{4} = \frac{7}{24}$.   Cu $\frac{7}{24}$.

This system is used to some extent, especially where most of the load is power; its use, however, is becoming less frequent, and in its place a three-wire single-phase system with separate three-phase motor mains is usually employed now for factory and mill work.

8. Three-wire Single-phase Lighting with Three-phase Power (Fig. 13).—*Lighting.*—Half-size neutral same as No. 2, therefore, copper economy: Cu $\frac{5}{16}$

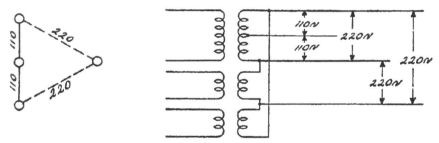

FIG. 13.—Single-phase lighting and three-phase power

Power.—Three-wire three-phase 220 volts; that is, the same as No. 5, but twice the voltage, thus one-quarter the copper of No. 5, or $\frac{1}{4}$ of $\frac{3}{4} = \frac{3}{16}$:   Cu $\frac{3}{16}$

This system is used very extensively.

The systems mostly used are:

No. 2.   Three-wire direct current or alternating-current single-phase.

No. 8.   Three-wire lighting, three-phase power. Less frequent.

No. 6.   Five-wire quarter-phase.

No. 7.   Four-wire three-phase.

As we have seen, the two-wire system is rather inefficient in copper. High efficiency requires the use of a third conductor, that is, the three-wire system, for direct current or single-phase alternating current

Three-wire polyphase systems, however, are inefficient in copper, as No 4 and No 5; and to reach approximately the same copper economy, as is reached by a three-wire system with direct current and single-phase alternating current, requires at least four wires with a polyphase system

That is, for equal economy in conductor material, the polyphase system requires at least one more conductor than the single-phase or the direct-current distribution system.

While the field of direct-current distribution is found in the interior of large cities, alternating current is used in smaller towns and villages and in the suburbs of large cities. In the latter, therefore, alternating current does the pioneer work. That is, the district is developed by alternating current, usually with overhead conductors, and when the load has become sufficiently large to warrant the establishment of converter substations, direct-current mains and feeders are laid under ground, the alternating-current distribution is abandoned, and the few alternating-current motors are replaced by direct-current motors. In the last years, however, considerable motor load has been developed in the alternating-current suburban distribution systems, fairly satisfactorily alternating-current elevator motors have been developed and introduced and the motor load has become so large as to make it economically difficult to replace the alternating-current motors by direct-current motors in changing the system to direct current; and it, therefore, appears that the distribution systems of large cities will be forced to maintain alternating-current distribution even in districts of such character as would make direct current preferable

As the result therefrom, direct-current distribution systems increase much less rapidly than alternating-current systems, and the alternating-current distribution thus is gaining ground, and new direct-current distribution systems are hardly ever established in cities, etc., but the direct-current generator finds its field in isolated stations, such as installed in office buildings, theatres, apartment houses, hotels, etc.

FOURTH LECTURE

LOAD FACTOR AND COST OF POWER

The cost of the power supplied at the customer's meter consists of three parts.

A   A fixed cost, that is, cost which is independent of the amount of power used, or the same whether the system is fully loaded or carries practically no load. Of this character, for instance, is the interest on the investment in the plant, the salaries of its officers, etc

B.   A cost which is proportional to the amount of power used. Such a proportional cost, for instance, is that of fuel in a steam plant.

C.   A cost depending on the reliability of service required, as the cost of keeping a steam reserve in a water-power transmission, or a storage-battery reserve in a direct-current distribution

Since of the three parts of the cost, only one, B, is proportional to the power used, hence constant per kilowatt output—the other two parts being independent of the output—hence the higher per kilowatt, the smaller a part of the capacity of the plant the output is, it follows that the cost of power delivered is a function of the ratio of the actual output of the plant, to the available capacity.

Interest on the investment of developing the water power or building the steam plant, the transmission lines, cables and distribution circuits, and depreciation are items of the character A, or fixed cost, since they are practically independent of the power which is produced and utilized

41

Fuel in a steam plant, oil, etc , are proportional costs, that is, essentially depending on the amount of power produced.

Salaries are fixed cost, A, labor, attendance and inspection are partly fixed cost A, partly proportional cost B— economy of operation requires, therefore, a shifting of as large a part thereof over into class B, by shutting down smaller substations during periods of light load, etc

Incandescent-lamp renewals, arc-lamp trimming, etc., are essentially proportional costs, B.

The reserve capacity of a plant, the steam reserve maintained at the receiving end of a transmission line, the difference in cost between a duplicate-pole line and a single-pole line with two circuits, the storage-battery reserve of the distribution system, the tie feeders between stations, etc , are items of the character C; that is, part of the cost insuring the reliability and continuity of power supply.

The greater the fixed cost A is, compared with the proportional cost B, the more rapidly the cost of power per kilowatt output increases with decreasing load.   Even in steam plants very frequently A is larger than B, that is, fuel, etc., not being the largest items of cost; in water-power plants A practically always is far larger than B   As result thereof, while water power may appear very cheap when considering only the proportional cost B—which is very low in most water powers—the fixed cost A usually is very high, due to the hydraulic development required   The difference in the cost of water power from that of steam power, therefore, is far less than appears at first.   As water power is usually transmitted over a long-distance line, while steam power is generated near the place of consumption, water power usually is far less reliable than steam power. To insure equal reliability, a water-power plant brings the item C, the reliability cost, very high in comparison with the reliability cost of a steam-power plant, since the possibility of a breakdown of a transmission line requires a steam reserve, and where absolute continuity of service is required, it requires also a storage battery, etc , so that on the basis of equal reliability of service, sometimes very little difference in cost exists between steam power and water power, unless the hydraulic development of the latter was very simple, and some very large steam-turbine plants are more economical in electric-power production, than most water-power plants.

The cost of electric power of different systems, therefore, is not directly comparable without taking into consideration the reliability of service and the character of the load

As a very large, and frequently even the largest part of the cost of power, is independent of the power utilized, and, therefore, rapidly increases with decreasing load on the system, the ratio of average power output to the available power capacity of the plant is of fundamental importance in the cost of power per kilowatt delivered. This ratio, of the average power consumption to the available power, or station capacity, has occasionally been called "load factor." This definition of the term "load factor" is, however, undesirable, since it does not take into consideration the surplus capacity of the station, which may have been provided for future extension, the reserve for insuring reliability C, etc.; and other such features which have no direct relation whatever to the character of the load.

Therefore, as load factor is generally understood the ratio of the average load to the maximum load, any excess of the station capacity beyond the maximum load is power which has not yet been sold, but which is still available for the market, or which is held in reserve for emergencies, is not charged against the load factor.

The cost of electric power essentially depends on the load factor. The higher the load factor, the less is the cost of the power, and a low load factor means an abnormally high cost per kilowatt. This is the case in steam power, and to a still greater extent in water power.

For the economical operation of a system, it therefore is of greatest importance to secure as high a load factor as possible, and consequently, the cost—and depending thereon the price—of electric power for different uses must

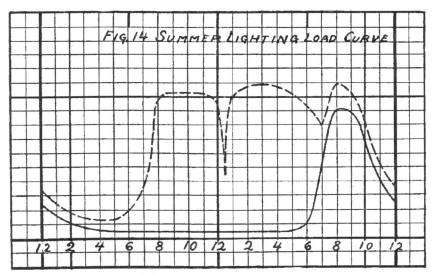

FIG. 14.—Summer lighting load curve and factory motor load curve.

be different if the load factors are different, and the higher the cost, the lower the load factor.

Electrochemical work gives the highest load factor, frequently some 90 per cent., while a lighting system shows the poorest load factor—in an alternating-current system without motor load occasionally it is as low as 10 to 20 per cent.

Defining the load factor as the ratio of the average to the maximum load, it is necessary to state over how long a time the average is extended; that is, whether daily, monthly or yearly load factor.

For instance, Fig. 14 shows an approximate load curve of a lighting circuit during a summer day; practically no load except for a short time during the evening, where a

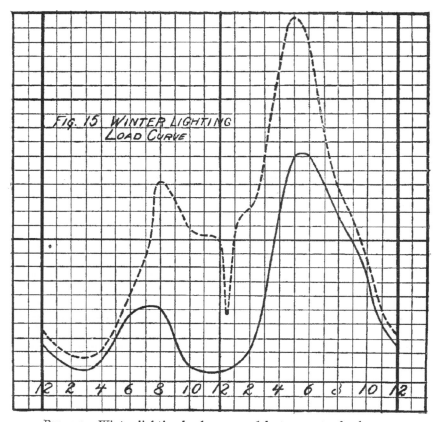

FIG. 15.—Winter lighting load curve and factory motor load curve

high peak is reached. The ratio of the average load to the maximum load during this day, or the daily load factor, is 22.8 per cent.

Fig. 15 shows an approximate lighting load curve for a winter day: a small maximum in the morning, and a very high evening maximum, of far greater width than the summer day curve, giving a daily load factor of 34 5 per cent.

During the year, the daily load curve varies between the extremes represented by Figs. 14 and 15, and the average annual load is therefore about midway between the average load of a summer day and that of a winter day. The maximum yearly load, however, is the maximum load during the winter day, and the ratio of average yearly load to maximum yearly load, or the yearly load factor of the lighting system, therefore is far lower than the daily load factor if we consider the average yearly load as the average between 14 and 15, the yearly load factor is only 23.6 per cent

One of the greatest disadvantages of lighting distribution, therefore, is the low yearly load factor, resulting from the summer load being so very far below the winter load; economy of operation, therefore, makes an increase of the summer lighting load very desirable. This has led to the development of spectacular lighting during the summer months, as represented by the various Luna Parks, Dreamlands, etc.

The load curve of a factory motor load is about the shape shown in Fig 16 fairly constant from the opening of the factories in the morning to their closing in the evening, with perhaps a drop of short duration during the noon hour, and a low extension in the evening, representing overtime work It gives a daily load factor of 49.5 per cent.

This load curve, superimposed upon the summer lighting curves, does not appreciably increases the maximum, but very greatly increases the average load, as shown by the dotted curve in Fig 14; and so improves the load factor, to 65 4 per cent —thereby greatly reducing the cost of the power to the station, in this way showing the great importance of securing a large motor load. During the winter months, however, the motor load overlaps the lighting maximum, as shown by the dotted curve in Fig. 15. This increases the maximum, and thereby increases the load factor less, only to 41.7 per cent. This is not so serious in the direct-current system with storage-battery reserve, as the overlap extends only for a short time, the overload being taken care of by storage batteries or by the overload

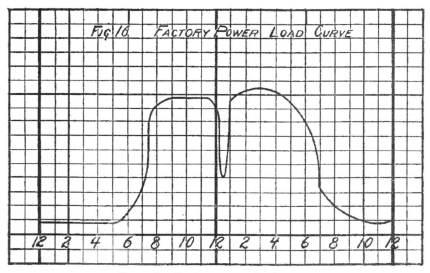

Fig. 16.—Factory power load curve.

capacity of generators and steam boilers; but where it is feasible, it is a great advantage if the users of motors can be induced to shut them down in winter with beginning darkness.

It follows herefrom, that additional load on the station during the peak of the load curve is very expensive, since it increases the fixed cost A and C, while additional load during the periods of light station load, only increases the proportional cost B; it therefore is desirable to discriminate against peak loads in favor of day loads and night loads.

For this purpose, two-rate meters have been developed, that is, meters which charge a higher price for power consumed during the peak of the load curve, than for power consumed during the light station loads. To even out load curves, and cut down the peak load, maximum-demand meters have been developed, that is, meters which charge for power somewhat in proportion to the load factor of the circuit controlled by the meter. Where the circuit is a lighting circuit, and the maximum demand therefore coincides with the station peak, this is effective, but on other classes of load the maximum-demand meters may discriminate against the station. For instance, a motor load giving a high maximum during some part of the day, and no load during the station peak, would be preferable to the station to a uniform load throughout the day, including the station peak, while the maximum-demand meter would discriminate against the former.

By a careful development of summer lighting loads and motor day loads, the load factors of direct-current distribution systems have been raised to very high values, 50 to 60 per cent , but in the average alternating-current system, the failure of developing a motor load frequently results in very unsatisfactory yearly load factors

The load curve of a railway circuit is about the shape of that shown in Fig. 17: a fairly steady load during the day, with a morning peak and an evening peak, occasionally a smaller noon peak and a small second peak later in the evening, then tapering down to a low value during the night The average load factor usually is far higher than in a lighting circuit, in Fig 17   54 3 per cent.

In defining the load factor, it is necessary to state not only the time over which the load is to be averaged, as a day, or a year, but also the length of time which the maximum load must last, to be counted. For instance, a short-circuit of a large motor during off-peak load, which is opened by the blowing of the fuses, may momentarily carry the load far beyond the station peak without being objectional. The minimum duration of maximum load, which is chosen in determining the load factor, is that which is permissible without being objectionable for the purpose for which the power is distributed. Thus in a lighting system, where voltage regulation is of foremost

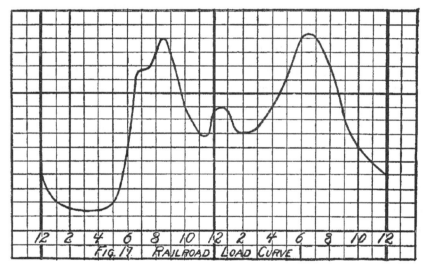

FIG. 17.—Railroad load curve.

importance, minutes may be chosen, and maximum load may be defined as the average load during that minute during which the load is a maximum; while in a railway system ½ hour may be used as a duration of maximum load, as a railway system is not so much affected by a drop of voltage due to overload, and an overload of less than ½ hour may be carried by the overload capacity of the generators and the heat storage of the steam boilers; so that a peak load requires serious consideration only when it exceeds ½ hour.

4

Where several classes of load are supplied by the same station, or even where the power supply to several distribution systems combines into one generating station, the average load factor of the total load usually is higher than the average of the load factors of the individual components of the load, due to the maximum peaks of the various loads not coinciding. In other words, the maximum load of the entire system is less than the sum of the maximum loads of the parts of the system. This ratio: sum of the maximum loads of all the parts of the system, divided by the maximum load of the entire system, is called the diversity factor of the total load.

The greater the diversity factor, the higher obviously is the load factor of the total system, and the higher, therefore, the economy, and the most economical operation, therefore, is afforded by those stations, which combine all the power supply, for lighting, power, railways, etc., into one hugh unified system. Such systems, as exemplified by the Commonwealth Edison Company of Chicago, thus are becoming of rapidly increasing importance in the electrical industry.

FIFTH LECTURE

LONG-DISTANCE TRANSMISSION

Three-phase is used altogether for long-distance transmission. Two-phase is not used any more, and direct current is being proposed, having been used abroad in a few cases; but due to the difficulty of generation and utilization, it is not probable that it will find any extended use, so that it does not need to be considered.

FREQUENCY

The frequency depends to a great extent on the character of the load, that is, whether the power is used for alternating-current distribution—60 cycles—or for conversion to direct current—25 cycles. For the transmission line, 25 cycles has the advantage that the charging current is less and the inductive drop is less, because charging current and inductance voltage are proportional to the frequency This advantage, however, is not so to handicap the use of 60 cycles even in very long transmission lines.

VOLTAGE

Eleven thousand to 13,000 volts and in a few instances even 22,000 volts have been used for shorter distances, as 10 to 20 miles, since this is about the highest voltage for which generators can be built; its use, therefore, saves the step-up transformers, that is, the generator feeds directly into the line and to the step-down transformers for the regular load However, the transmission range of these voltages is so low, and the design of the high-voltage generator at such disadvantage by localized heating due

51

to the heavy insulation required, and by corona in the generator coils, that the general tendency of the industry is away from directly generating the transmission voltage.

The next step is 30,000 volts; that is, 33,000 volts at the generator, 30,000 at the receiving end of the line. No intermediate voltages between this and the voltage for which generators can be wound is used, as 30,000 volts does not yet offer any insulator troubles; but line insulators can be built at moderate cost for this voltage, and as step-up transformers have to be used, it is not worth while to consider any lower voltage than 33,000 volts. This voltage transmits economically up to distances of 50 to 60 miles.

Forty thousand to 44,000 volts is the next step. it was the highest transmission voltage, at which reliable operation could be assured with the former or pin type of insulator: a few 60,000-volt systems were tried, but were not very successful regarding reliability.

The development of the suspension insulator entirely changed the situation: it made it possible to insulate with a very high safety factor at moderate cost practically any voltage. The line insulator thereby vanished as limitation of the voltage permissible in transmission lines, and lines of 100,000 volts and over have become quite frequent, gave very successful operation, and the only voltage limit in transmission now is the corona loss from the line conductor, but not the line insulator

For these high-voltage transmissions, steel-tower lines are almost exclusively used.

The cost of a long-distance transmission line depends on the voltage used.

The cost of line conductors decreases with the square of the voltage.

At twice the voltage, twice the line drop can be allowed

with the same loss; at twice the voltage the current is only half for the same power, and twice the drop with half the current gives four times the resistance, that is, one-quarter the conductor section and cost

The cost of line insulators increases with increase of voltage. The cost of pole line increases with increase of voltage, since greater distance between the conductors is necessary and so longer poles or higher towers, longer cross arms, and heavier construction, and not so many circuits can be carried on the same pole line. In general, a good safe margin is given by allowing 1 foot for every 10,000 volts between the conductors.

The lower the voltage, the greater in general is the reliability of operation, since a larger margin of safety can be allowed. However, the difference is not great, and in the contrary, extremely high-voltage lines have shown a considerable immunity from lightning disturbances, that is, their normal insulation is sufficient to protect them from most lightning effects

Since a part of the cost of the transmission line decreases, another part increases with the voltage, a certain voltage will be most economical

Lower voltage increases the cost of the conductor, higher voltage increases the cost of insulators and line construction, and may decrease the reliability

The most economical voltage of a transmission line varies with the cost of copper. When copper is very high, higher voltages are more economical than when copper is low. The same applies to aluminum, since the price of aluminum has been varied with that of copper

Aluminum generally is used as stranded conductor. In the early days single wire gave much trouble by flaws in the wire Aluminum expands more than copper with temperature changes, and so when installing the line in summer, a greater sag must be allowed than with copper, otherwise it stretches so tight in winter that it may tear apart. Aluminum also is more difficult to join together, since it cannot be welded.

For the same conductivity an aluminum line has about twice the size, but one-half of the weight of a copper conductor, and costs a little less; on the other hand, copper has a permanent value, while the price of aluminum may sometime drop altogether, as the metal has no intrinsic value, being one of the most common constituents of the surface of the earth, and its cost is merely that of its separation or reduction

LOSSES IN LINE DUE TO HIGH VOLTAGE

The loss in the line by brush discharge or corona effect is nothing up to a certain voltage, but at a certain voltage it begins and very rapidly increases.

The voltage at which the loss by corona begins in a transmission line is where the air at and near the surface of the conductor, and up to a small distance from the conductor, has broken down, becomes conducting and thus luminous.

There is thus a voltage e_o—usually not far from 100 kilovolts (1 kilovolt = 1000 volts) under industrial transmission-line conditions—at which the breakdown gradient of air, 21 kilovolts (alternating effective) per centimeter (53,000 volts per inch) is reached at the surface of the transmission wire.

This voltage, e_o, the "disruptive critical voltage" of the line, is given by

$$e_o = 84 \ r\delta \ \log \frac{s}{r} \ \text{kilovolts} \ \text{alternating between}$$

three-phase lines

where

r = radius of conductor in centimeters

s = spacing between conductor centers in centimeters.

δ = air density factor = 1 at 25°C. and 76-centimeter barometer, thus

$$\delta = \frac{3.92b}{273 + t}$$

where t = temperature, in degrees C., and b = barometer, in centimeters of mercury.

(The log is the common logarithm.)

This applies only to round conductors with smooth polished surface, if the surface of the conductor is roughened or weathered, e_o is about 5 per cent. lower.

If the conductor is a seven-strand cable, with r as the outer or overall radius, e_o is about 15 per cent. lower

However, no appreciable loss occurs yet at this voltage, e_o. Only at a little higher voltage, e_v, the "visual critical voltage" of the line, when the breakdown of the air has extended from the wire a little ways, an appreciable loss begins, and the conductor becomes luminous in the dark.

The visual critical voltage is given by·

$$e_v = e_o \left\{ 1 + \frac{0 \ 3}{\sqrt{\delta r}} \right\}$$

While thus a material loss begins only at e_v, and not at e_o, the amount of loss, where it occurs, is proportional to the square of the excess voltage over e_o, and is given by the expression

$$p = \frac{244}{\delta} (f + 25) \sqrt{\frac{r}{s}} (e - e_o)^2 \ 10^{-5} \ kilowatts$$

per kilometer of three-phase line (three conductors). Where:

f = frequency,

e = operating voltage between three-phase lines,

The corona loss thus increases with the frequency, and very rapidly increases with the voltage and it therefore is not safe to materially exceed the voltage e_o in transmission lines.

e_o and e_v depend on size of conductor, and distance from return conductor, and are proportional to the air density, that is, at higher temperature and lower barometric pressure, e_o and e_v are lower. Thus at an altitude where the barometer reads 24 inches—about 6000 feet elevation—corona begins already at $24/30 = 0 8$ times the voltage at which it begins at the sea level

Thus lines traversing high altitudes are liable to be much more affected by corona losses, and the question of altitude requires serious consideration.

In addition to the normal corona loss, there may be very material additional corona losses already at lower voltages, under conditions of heavy rain, and especially snow storms.

In general, it may probably be said that with the sizes of wires, and distances between wires usual in long-distance transmissions, corona losses are rarely to be feared at line voltages below 100,000, but at line voltages above 100,-000, the question of corona on the transmission line, and the possible amount of loss caused thereby, should be investigated

In Fig 18 are shown as ordinates the line voltages e_v (voltage between three-phase lines), at which luminosity by corona begins, for different spacings of the line conductors as abscissæ, and for different conductor diameters, at sea level, that is, air density $\delta = 1$.

In high-potential transformers in the coils usually no corona effects occur, because the diameter of the coil or the thickness is large enough, but the leads connecting the coils with each other and with the outside, if not chosen very large in diameter, may give corona effects and so break down.

In a line or transformer, if one side is grounded, the other side has full voltage against ground, and so may give corona

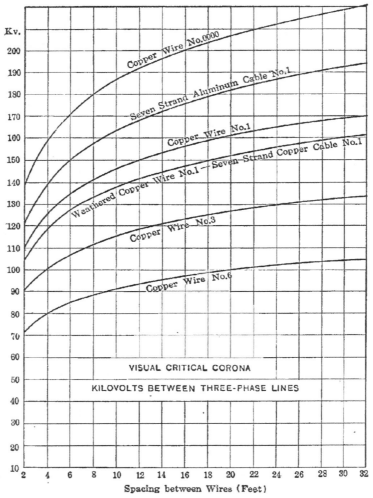

FIG. 18.—Corona voltage of three-phase lines.

effects and break down; while if not grounded, both sides have half voltage against ground and so give no corona effect. In the first case, the line or transformer so may break down, although the potential differences between the terminals are no greater than in the second case.

For instance, in a 200,000-volt transformer or line, from each terminal to ground are 100,000 volts, and if the conductor diameter is ½-inch, no corona effects occur. If now one terminal is grounded, the other terminal has 200,000 volts to ground and so at ½-inch diameter gives corona effects, that is, glow and streamers which may destroy the insulating material or produce high-frequency oscillations

At very high voltages it is, therefore, necessary to have the system statically balanced or symmetrical, that is, have the same potential differences from all the conductors to the ground.

In circuits inductively connected (that is by transformation) to circuits of higher voltage, such static unbalancing of the higher voltage circuit may endanger the lower voltage circuit, especially if the latter is isolated from ground.

Suppose in a 100,000-volt system, one line grounds. The average potential difference of this system, and thus also of the high-potential coils of the step-down transformers, is the Y-voltage, or 58,000 volts against ground. Even if the step-down transformer is perfectly isolated, there is then a path to ground, of the 58,000 volts unbalanced voltage, over two capacities in series: the capacity from the high-potential transformer winding as one condenser plate, to the low-potential or secondary transformer winding as other condenser plate, and from the low-potential transformer winding or secondary circuit, to ground. Depending on the two capacities, the voltages thus divide, but if the normal voltage of the secondary circuit is low, for instance 2200 or 6600 volts, even a small part of the static voltage of 58,000, on the condenser from the secondary to ground, may be destructive by causing continual spark discharges, finally followed by rupture.

Some transformer connections, as open delta, give such static unbalancing even without ground on the primary

It follows herefrom, that any secondary circuit, connected by transformation with a primary circuit of much higher voltage, must be protected against static voltages induced by the primary winding and comparable in magnitude with the primary voltage.

Any overvoltage protective device, as lightning arrester, or a grounding of the secondary circuit, gives such protection; and even a very high-resistance path to ground— as a high-resistance rod with some spark gaps in series or so-called "static discharger"—affords complete protection, as the power, which has to be discharged, is extremely small, being due to static induction through the transformer, and the only danger is the disruptive effect of its high voltage.

Any electric circuit, and so also the transmission line, contains inductance and capacity, and, therefore, stores energy as electromagnetic energy in the magnetic field due to the current, and as electrostatic energy, or electrostatic charge, due to the voltage

If:

$$e = \text{voltage}, \quad C = \text{capacity}$$
$$i = \text{current}, \quad L = \text{inductance}.$$

the electrostatic energy is·

$$\frac{e^2 C}{2}$$

and the electromagnetic energy:

$$\frac{i^2 L}{2}$$

In a high-potential transmission line both energies are of about the same magnitude, and the energy can, therefore, seesaw between the two forms and thereby produce oscillations and surges resulting in the production of high voltages, which are not liable to occur in circuits in which one of the forms of stored energy is small compared with the other.

In distribution systems up to 2200 volts and even somewhat higher, the electrostatic energy is still negligible and only the electromagnetic energy appreciable

In static machines the electrostatic energy is appreciable, but the electromagnetic energy negligible.

LINES AND TRANSFORMERS

At voltages above 25,000 step-up and step-down transformers are always used, which are, therefore, a part of the high-potential circuit.

Three-phase is always used in the transmission line.

Some of the available transformer connections are given in Figs. 19 and 20.

Grounding the neutral of the system has the advantage of maintaining static balance and so avoiding oscillations and disturbances in case of an accidental static unbalancing, as for instance, the grounding of one line   It has the disadvantage that a ground on one circuit is a short-circuit and so shuts down the circuit, while with the ungrounded circuit, the grounding of one line merely produces a static unbalancing, which can be taken care of by protective devices and larger margin in the insulators   The relation between transmission lines with grounded neutral and lines with ungrounded neutral thus is essentially that between cheapness and between reliability where reliability is of foremost importance and justifies the somewhat higher cost of better insulation, the isolated delta system of the ungrounded transmission is preferable; where

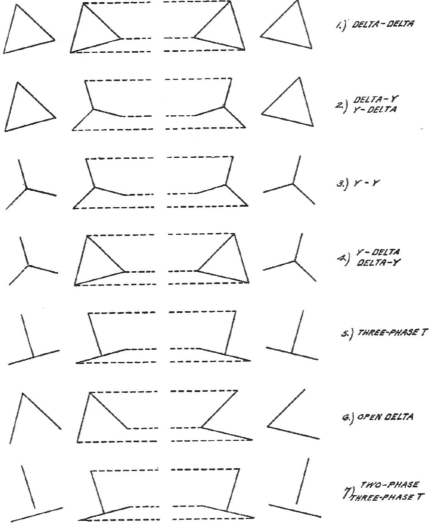

FIG. 19.—Transformer connections.

cheapness of construction is of the greatest importance, even at the sacrifice of some reliability, the grounded *Y*-system, that is, system with grounded neutral is indicated.

In connections 1, 4 and 6 no neutral is available for grounding and so three separate transformers have to be installed in *Y*-connection for getting the neutral.

In connection 2 and 3 the neutral can be brought out from the transformer neutral.

In the *T*-connection 5 and 7, the neutral is brought out from a point at one-third of the teaser transformer winding.

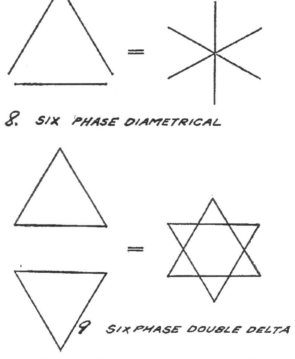

8. SIX PHASE DIAMETRICAL

9 SIX PHASE DOUBLE DELTA

Fig. 20.—Six-phase transformer connections.

In general the connection 1 is the safest and therefore is preferable, as every transformer coil connects between points of fixed voltage, the lines, and therefore no excess voltages are liable to appear on a transformer coil, as may in cases where high-potential coils of different transformers are in series with each other, in the *Y* and the *T*-connection, as will be seen later.

Assuming the line properly installed and insulated, breakdowns may occur, either from mechanical accidents or by high voltages appearing in the line.

HIGH-VOLTAGE DISTURBANCES IN TRANSMISSION LINES

These may be:

A. Of fundamental frequency, that is, the same frequency as the alternating-current machine circuit.

B. Some higher harmonic of the generator wave, that is, some odd multiple of the generator frequency

C. Of frequencies entirely independent of the generator, or of a frequency which originates in the circuit, that is, high-frequency oscillations as arcing grounds, etc.

If a capacity is in series with an inductance, as the line capacity and the line inductance, the capacity reactance and the inductive reactance are opposed to each other, if they happened to be equal they would neutralize each other, the current would depend on the resistance only and therefore be very large, and with this very large current passing through the inductance and capacity, the voltage at the inductance and at the capacity would be very high.

For instance, if we have 20,000 volts supplied to a circuit having a resistance of 10 ohms and a capacity reactance of 1000 ohms, then the total impedance of the circuit is $\sqrt{10^2 + 1000^2} = 1000$ and the current in the circuit $\frac{20,000}{1000} = 20$ amperes.

If now in addition to the 10 ohms resistance and 1000 ohms capacity reactance, the circuit contains 1000 ohms inductive reactance, the total reactance of the circuit is $1000 - 1000 = 0$ ohms, and the impedance is the same as the resistance, or 10 ohms. The current therefore $\frac{e}{z} = \frac{e}{r} =$

2000 amperes, and the voltage at the capacity, therefore, is: capacity reactance times amperes = 2,000,000 volts, and the same voltage exists at the inductive reactance

These voltages are far beyond destruction That is, if in a circuit of low resistance and high capacity reactance, a high inductive reactance is put in series with the capacity reactance, excessive voltages are produced.

In a transmission line the capacity of the line consumes for instance 10 per cent. of full-load current, that is, full-load voltage sends only 10 per cent. of full-load current through the capacity To send full-load current through the capacity so would require 10 times full-load voltage.

With a line reactance of 20 per cent , 20 per cent or ⅕ of full-load voltage sends full-load current through the inductive reactance, while 10 times full-load voltage is required by the capacity reactance, the capacity reactance, therefore, is about 50 times larger than the inductive reactance at the generator frequency and, therefore, cannot build up with it to excessive voltages; but to get resonance with the fundamental frequency requires an inductive reactance about 50 times greater than the line reactance.

The only reactance in the system which is large enough to build up with the capacity reactance is the open-circuit reactance of the transformers. This is of about the same size as the capacity reactance, since a transformer at open circuit and full voltage takes about 10 per cent. of full-load current, and the capacity reactance also takes about 10 per cent. of full-load current, in moderately short lines.

If, therefore, a high-potential coil of a transformer at open secondary circuit is connected in series with a transmission line, destructive voltages may be produced, by the reactance of the transformer building up with the line capacity. In those transformer connections in which several high-potential coils of different transformers are connected between the transmission wires, this may occur if the low-tension coil of one of the transformers accidentally opens and the high-potential coil of this transformer then acts as inductive reactance in series with the line capacity in the circuit of the other transformer.

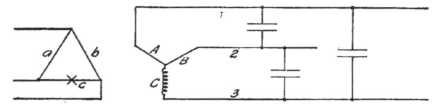

FIG. 21.—Fundamental frequency resonance.

This may occur for instance in transformer connection 2, Fig. 19, if as shown in Fig 21, the low-tension coil *c* opens. Then the high-tension coil *C* is an inductive reactance in series with the line capacity from 3 to 1, energized by transformer *A*; and *C* is a high inductive reactance in series with the line capacity from 3 to 2 in a circuit of

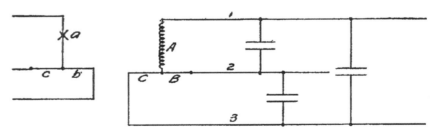

FIG. 22.—Fundamental frequency resonance.

voltage *B*. That is, from 3 to 1 and from 3 to 2 excessive voltages are produced. So also in *T*-connection, Fig. 22, if for instance the low-tension coil *a* opens, the corresponding high-tension coil *A* is a high inductive reactance in series with the line capacities in a circuit of the voltages of the two halves, *B* and *C*, of the other transformer, and

5

excessive voltages, therefore, appear from 1 to 2 and from 1 to 3.

This danger of excessive voltages by the accidental opening of a transformer low-tension coil does not exist in delta-connection, since in this always only one transformer connects from line to line. It is greatly reduced since the use of triple-pole switches became general; and is very much less where several sets of transformers are used in multiple, since even if in one set a low-tension coil opens, the other sets maintain the voltage triangle

Especially dangerous in this respect, therefore, is the *L*-connection No. 6, since in this case, when using two transformers in open delta, for smaller systems only one set is installed and an accident to one of the transformers causes excessive voltages between its line and the two other lines

The open-circuit reactance of the transformer is the only reactance high enough to give destructive voltages at generator frequency, and in high-potential disturbances, the transformer connections should first be carefully investigated to see whether this has occurred.

However, a considerable and destructive voltage rise of fundamental frequency may occur by the combination of a partial resonance rise, as discussed above, with over-excitation of the generators and increase of speed by the racing of the turbines. For instance, consider a very long high-voltage transmission line—of 150 to 200 miles and 110,000 to 150,000 volts, thus a capacity current of 50 per cent. or more of full-load current Suppose now a short-circuit of appreciable resistance, that is, high power consumption, occurs at the end of the lines: to maintain the voltage, the automatic regulators on the generators increase the field excitation to the maximum. To maintain the speed, the turbine governors open the gates wide.

Suppose now the short-circuit is suddenly opened. before the water gates can shut off, the turbines may have increased 50 per cent. in speed; the field excitation would give a voltage far above normal at normal speed, and still 50 per cent. higher at the speed of the racing turbines, and adding thereto the voltage rise in the line capacity, it follows that under such conditions a voltage rise, at normal frequency and backed by the machine power, may occur of 100 per cent or more. Such systems thus make voltage control by synchronous condensers at the receiving end desirable, if not necessary.

SIXTH LECTURE

HIGHER HARMONICS OF THE GENERATOR WAVE

The open-circuit reactance of the transformer is the only reactance high enough to give resonance with the line capacity at fundamental frequency.

All other reactances are too low for this.

Since, however, the inductive reactance increases and the capacity reactance decreases proportionally to the frequency, the two reactances come nearer together for higher frequency, that is, for the higher harmonics of the generator wave, and for some of the higher harmonics of the generator wave resonance rise of voltage so may occur between the line capacity and the circuit inductance.

The origin and existence of higher harmonics, therefore, bears investigation in transformers, transmission lines and cable systems

ORIGIN OF HIGHER HARMONICS

Higher harmonics may originate in synchronous machines, as generators, synchronous motors and converters, and in transformers.

These two classes of higher harmonics are very different. The former have constant-potential character; the latter, constant-current character; their cure and prevention, therefore, must be different, and the method of elimination of one may be very harmful with the other type of harmonics. For instance, the voltage produced by a constant-current harmonic as coming from a transformer is eliminated by short-circuit, as produced by delta connec-

68

tion on one side of the transformer. Short-circuiting a generator harmonic, however, gives large short-circuit currents, due to the constant-potential character, and is therefore dangerous.

HIGHER HARMONICS OF SYNCHRONOUS MACHINES

In synchronous machines, as alternating-current generators, the higher harmonics are

At No Load.—*First.*—The distribution of magnetism in the air gap depends on the shape of the field poles, it is not a sine wave, neither is the e.m.f. induced by it in an armature conductor a sine wave.

Since there are a number of conductors in series on the armature, the voltage wave is more evened out than that of a single conductor, but still it is not a sine wave, that is, contains harmonics of which the third is the lowest.

Second.—The change of magnetic flux by the passage of open armature slots over the field pole produces harmonics of e m f ; that is, when a large open armature slot stands in front of the field pole, the magnetic reluctance is high; the magnetism is lower than when no slot is in front of the field pole; that is, by the passage of the armature slots the field magnetism pulsates, the more so the larger the slots and the fewer they are

If there are n slots per pole, this produces the two harmonics $2n - 1$ and $2n + 1$.

At Load.—*Third.*—The armature reaction of a single-phase machine pulsates between zero at zero current and a maximum at maximum current

The resultant armature reaction of a polyphase machine is constant, but locally there is a pulsation making as many cycles per pole as there are phases.

Since the field magnetism under load is due to the combination of field excitation and armature reaction, the pulsation of armature reaction therefore causes a pulsation of field magnetism, and thereby higher harmonics of the e m f. wave

If m = number of phases, the higher harmonics: $2m - 1$ and $2m + 1$ are produced.

Fourth.—The terminal voltage under load is the resultant of the induced e.m.f. and the e.m.f consumed by the reactance of the armature circuit; that is, the reactance produced by the magnetic flux produced by the armature current in the armature iron   This armature reactance is not constant, but periodically varies, more or less, with double frequency; that is, when the armature coil is in front of the field pole its magnetic circuit is different than when it is between the field poles, and the reactance therefore is different.

This pulsation of armature reactance produces the third harmonic, since it is of double frequency.

The most common and prominent harmonic so is the third harmonic in a synchronous machine.

These harmonics of synchronous machines are induced e.m.fs., that is, constant-potential or approximately so.

HIGHER HARMONICS OF TRANSFORMERS

In a transformer the wave of e.m.f. depends on that of the magnetism and *vice versa*.   That is, with a sine wave of e.m f., the magnetism must also be a sine wave, and if the magnetism is not a sine wave, but contains higher harmonics, the e.m.f. is not a sine wave, both contains the harmonics induced by the harmonics of magnetism

The exciting current of the transformer depends on the magnetism by the hysteresis cycle; if the magnetism is a sine wave, the exciting current, therefore, cannot be a sine wave, but must contain higher harmonics—mainly the third harmonic, which reaches 20 to 30 per cent. of the fundamental, or even more at saturation.

In a transformer, e.m.f. and exciting current, therefore, cannot both be sine waves, but a sine wave of e.m.f. requires an exciting current containing a third harmonic; and a sine wave of exciting current in a transformer or reactive coil thus produces a third harmonic of e.m f.

If, therefore, in a transformer the third harmonic is suppressed, and if this third harmonic should have been 20 per cent. of the fundamental, then its suppression produces a third harmonic of magnetism of 20 per cent. in the opposite direction. A third harmonic of magnetism, however, of 20 per cent , induces a third harmonic of e m f. of $3 \times 20 = 60$ per cent., the e.m f. being proportional to magnetism and frequency

In three-phase transformers, this, however, is the case only if the magnetic circuit is arranged so that the flux of each phase closes its circuit without passing through another phase, so-called shell-type transformers. If, however, the magnetic fluxes of the three-phase transformer are interlinked so that each magnetic circuit interlinks with two phases—so-called core-type transformers—no triple-frequency flux can exist in a closed magnetic circuit, since the phases neutralize, and the triple-frequency fluxes have open magnetic circuits, thus usually are very small, and the triple-frequency voltages thus negligible.

The third harmonic of exciting current is positive at the maximum of magnetism, and the third harmonic of magnetism is negative at the maximum, hence is zero and rising at the zero of the magnetism, and at this moment the e.m.f. induced by the third harmonic and by the fundamental, therefore, are both maxima and in the same direction,

that is, add. The suppression of the third harmonic
of exciting current thus produces a very high third harmonic
of e.m.f., which greatly increases the maximum e.m.f.;
that is, the e.m.f. wave is very low for a large part of the
cycle and then rises to a very high peak, as shown in Fig. 23;
and the maximum e.m.f. may exceed that of a sine wave by
50 per cent. and more, thus giving high insulation stress
and the possibility of resonance voltages.

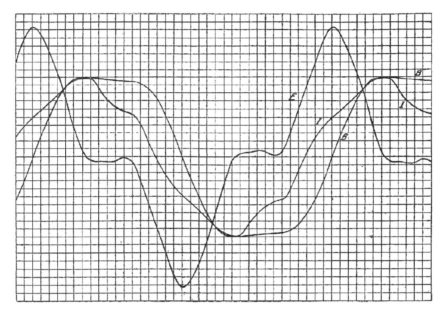

FIG. 23.—Wave distortion by suppression of third harmonic in transformer.

EFFECTS OF HIGHER HARMONICS

In a three-phase system the three phases are 120° apart,
and their third harmonics are 3 × 120° = 360° apart, that
is, in phase with each, and for the third harmonic the three-
phase system therefore is a single-phase system.

In a balanced three-phase system, the third harmonics
cannot exist in the voltages between the lines and in the
line currents, if there is no return over the neutral.   The

three voltages between lines, from 1 to 2, 2 to 3, and 3 to 1, must add up to zero, but since the third harmonics would be in phase with each other, they would not add up to zero, therefore they cannot exist. The three currents, if there is no return over the neutral or the ground, must add up to zero; and since their third harmonics must be in phase with each other, they must be absent In a balanced three-phase system, third harmonics can exist only in the voltage from line to neutral or *Y*-voltage, in the current from line to line or delta current, and in the line current only if there is a neutral return or ground return to the generator neutral or transformer neutral.

In a three-phase generator, if the e m f. of one phase contains a third harmonic, as is usually the case, then by connecting the three phases in delta connection, the third harmonics of the generator e.m.fs. are short-circuited and so produce a triple-frequency current circulating in the generator delta. This triple-frequency circulating current can be measured by connecting an ammeter in one corner of the generator delta, and the sum of voltages of the three third harmonics can be measured by putting a voltmeter in a corner of the generator delta. This local current in the generator winding is the triple-frequency voltage divided by the generator impedance (the stationary impedance, at triple frequency, but not the synchronous impedance, since the latter includes armature reaction). In generators of low impedance or close regulation, as turbine alternators, this local current may be far more than full-load current; delta connection of generator windings therefore is unsafe. As a result, generator windings are almost always connected in *Y*. Even with delta connection of generator windings no triple frequency appears at the terminals, since its voltage disappears by short-circuit.

If the generator winding is connected in Y, the triple-frequency voltages from terminal to neutral are in phase with each other, that is, in a three-phase Y-connected generator, a single-phase voltage of triple frequency exists between the neutral and all three terminals, and the neutral therefore is not a true neutral. Between the lines no triple-frequency voltage exists, since from terminal to neutral and from neutral to the other terminal the two third harmonics are in opposition and so neutralize.

This third harmonic between generator neutral and line must be kept in mind, since when large it may produce dangerous voltages by resonance with the line capacity.

When the generator neutral is grounded, the potential difference from line to ground is not line voltage divided by $\sqrt{3}$, that is, the true Y-voltage of the system, but superimposed upon it is this single-phase triple-frequency voltage, and the voltage from line to ground, especially its maximum, may be greatly increased, thus increasing the insulation strain. For this single-phase voltage all three lines go together, and so may cause static induction on other circuits, as telephone lines A circuit of this single-phase triple-frequency voltage then exists from the generator neutral over the inductance of all three generator circuits in multiple, and over the capacity of all three lines to ground, back to the generator neutral, that is, we have capacity and inductance in series in a circuit of the triple harmonic, and if capacity and inductance are high enough, we may get a dangerous voltage rise.

In this case of grounded generator neutral, if the primary neutral of the Y-connected step-down transformers is grounded also, and the low-tension side of these transformers connected in Y, the third harmonic of the generator has no path; the current produced by it would have to return over the open-circuit reactance of the step-down transformer, and is limited thereby to a negligible value

If, however, the secondaries of the step-down transformers are connected in delta, so that the third harmonic can circulate in the secondary delta, the third harmonic can flow through the transformer primary by inducing an opposite current in the secondary; in this case the step-down transformer short-circuits the third harmonic of the generator. Grounding the primary neutral of step-down transformers with grounded generator neutral, therefore, is permissible only if the transformer secondaries are also connected in Y. With delta-connected transformer secondaries, however, it is not safe to ground the generator neutral and transformer neutral; since this produces a triple-frequency current in generator, line and transformer; and even if the generator reactance is so high that the generator is not harmed by this current, it may burn out the transformer, and probably will do so if the transformer is small compared with the generator.

This, therefore, is a case where delta connection of the transformer secondaries does not eliminate the trouble from the third harmonic, but makes it worse.

In other words, delta connection of at least one side of the transformer eliminates the third harmonic resulting from the transformer, but is not safe if it lets the third harmonic of the generator flow.

The triple-frequency voltage from line to ground would be eliminated by short-circuiting it in this manner, by Y-delta connection of step-down transformer with grounded generator and transformer neutral, and static induction on other circuits so would disappear; but we get magnetic induction from the three triple-frequency single-phase currents which now flow over the lines to the ground.

If the generator neutral is not grounded, it is safe to ground transformer neutrals. With ungrounded generator neutral, a triple-frequency voltage can be measured by voltmeter, which then appears between generator neutral and ground; this voltage under unfavorable conditions, may give insulation strains in the generator by resonance rise in the circuit from generator neutral over triple-frequency voltage, generator inductance, capacity from line to ground and capacity from ground to generator winding in series.

In this case the capacity is much lower and the power therefore much less, that is, less danger exists.

When running two or more three-phase generators in parallel, with grounded neutrals:

(a) If the generators have different third harmonics, these harmonics are short-circuited from neutral over generator to the other generator and back to neutral; a triple-frequency current thus flows between the generators, that is, the current between the generators can never be made to disappear.

That is, for the third harmonic, the two generators are two single-phase machines of different voltage, having the neutral as one terminal and the three three-phase terminals as the other single-phase terminal

(b) With two identical generators running in multiple, if the excitation is identically the same, no current flows between the grounded neutrals. If the excitation of the two generators is different, one is overexcited the other is underexcited (that is, one carries leading, the other lagging current) then a triple-frequency current flows between the neutrals of identical generators. Since in parallel operation the terminal voltages are in phase, if by difference of excitation the two terminal voltages have a different lag behind the induced e.m.fs., the third harmonics, which lag three times as much as the fundamentals, cannot be in phase in the two machines, and thus triple-frequency current flows between the machines.

In machines of very low reactance as turbo-alternators, even small differences in excitation of identical machines with grounded neutral may sometimes cause very large neutral currents.

In parallel operation of three-phase machines with grounded neutral, machines of different wave shapes frequently cannot be run together at all without excessive neutral currents, and the ground has to be taken off of one of the machine types.

Even with identical machines, care has to be taken in keeping the same excitation so that it is frequently undesirable to ground all the neutrals, but only the neutral of one machine is grounded and the other machine neutrals are left isolated. In this case, provisions must be made to ground the neutral of some other machine, if the first one is out of service. The best way is, when grounding generator neutrals, to ground through a separate resistance for every generator and to choose this resistance so high as to limit the neutral current, but still low enough so that in case of a ground on one phase, enough current flows over the neutral to open the circuit-breaker of the grounded phase.

The use of a resistance in the generator neutral is very desirable also, since it eliminates the danger of a high-frequency oscillation between line and ground through the generator reactance in the path of the third harmonic, by damping the oscillation in the resistance For this reason, the resistance should be non-inductive. To ground the generator neutral through a reactance is very dangerous since it intensifies the danger of a resonance voltage rise.

In grounding the generator neutral, special care is necessary to get perfect contact, since an arc or loose contact would generate a high frequency in the circuit of the third harmonic and so may lead to a higher-frequency oscillation between line and ground.

SEVENTH LECTURE

HIGH FREQUENCY OSCILLATIONS, SURGES AND IMPULSES

In an electric circuit, in addition to the power consumption by the resistance of the lines, an energy storage occurs as electrostatic energy, or electrostatic charge due to the voltage on the line (capacity); and as electromagnetic energy, or magnetic field of the current in the line (inductance) In the long-distance transmission line, both amounts of stored energy are very considerable, and of about equal magnitude, the former varying with the voltage, the latter with the current in the line. Any change of the voltage on the line, or the current in the line, or the relation between voltage and current, therefore requires a corresponding change of the stored energy; that is, a readjustment of the stored energy in the system, the electrostatic energy $\dfrac{e^2C}{2}$ and the electromagnetic energy $\dfrac{i^2L}{2}$, from that previous to the changed circuit conditions. This readjustment occurs by an oscillation, that is, a series of waves of voltage and of current, which gradually decreases in intensity, that is, dies out. Very frequently such an oscillation or stationary electric wave is preceded by an impulse or traveling wave, which rushes along the circuit from the source of disturbance, and by reflection from the end of the circuit, etc., develops into the oscillation. Such impulses or traveling waves if of very high frequency may pass over the circuit without resulting in an appreciable oscillation, and may not even be periodic, but single unidirectional impulses.

79

These oscillating voltages and currents are the result of the readjustment of the stored energy of the circuit to a sudden change of conditions, and are dependent upon the stored energy of the circuit, but not upon the generator frequency or wave shape; therefore they occur in the same manner, and are of the same frequency, in a 25-cycle system as in a 60-cycle system, or a high-potential direct-current transmission; and occur with sine waves of generator voltage equally as with distorted generator waves. While the power of these oscillations ultimately comes from the generators, it is not the generator wave nor one of its harmonics which builds up, as discussed in the previous lectures; but the generator merely supplies the energy, which is stored as electrostatic charge of the capacity and as magnetic field of the inductance, and the readjustment of this stored energy to the change of circuit conditions then gives the oscillation

These oscillating voltages and currents, adding to the generator voltage and current, thus increase the voltage and the current the more, the greater the intensity of the oscillation, and so may lead to destructive voltages.

Obviously, the intensity of the oscillation, that is, its voltage and current, are the greater, the greater or more abrupt the change was in the circuit, which caused the oscillation by requiring a readjustment of the energy storage. The greatest change in a circuit, however, is the change from short-circuit to open circuit, and the instantaneous opening of a short-circuit on a transmission line—as it occasionally occurs by the sudden rupture of a short-circuiting arc—therefore gives rise to the most powerful, and thereby most destructive oscillation.

The wave length of oscillation thus depends on the length of the circuit in which the stored energy readjusts itself. For instance, in the short-circuit oscillation of the system, the wave extends over the entire circuit, including generators and transformers, and the entire circuit so epresents one wave, or one-half wave, that is, the wave-length is very considerable. If the readjustment of stored energy takes place only over a section of the circuit, the wave length is shorter. For instance, if by a thunder cloud a static charge is induced on the transmission line, and by a lightning flash in the cloud, the cloud discharges, the electrostatic charge induced by it on the line is set free and dissipates by an oscillation. In this case, the length of section on which an abnormal charge existed—1 mile for instance—is a half wave of the oscillation, and the complete wave length would thus be 2 miles. Or, if a momentary discharge occurs over a lightning arrester to ground, the wave length may be only a few feet

The velocity with which the electric wave travels in an overhead line is practically the velocity of light, or about 188,000 miles per second it would be exactly the velocity of light, except that by the resistance of the line conductor the velocity is very slightly reduced. In an underground cable, by the high capacity of the cable insulation, the velocity of wave travel is greatly reduced, to about 50 to 70 per cent. of that of light.

From the wave length and the velocity follows the duration or time of one wave, and thereby the frequency of the oscillation. For instance, in the wave of 2 miles' length resulting from induction by a thunder cloud, as discussed above, the duration of the wave, or the time it takes to travel the wave length of 2 miles, at 188,000 miles per second velocity, is $\dfrac{2}{188,000} = \dfrac{1}{94,000}$ second, and thus, during 1 second, 94,000 waves would pass, that is, the frequency is

6

94,000 cycles. Or, if a transmission line of 80 miles'
length short-circuits at one end, and then disconnects at
the other end by the opening of the circuit-breaker, in the
oscillation produced thereby the circuit is one-half wave.
As the length of the circuit is $2 \times 80 = 160$ miles—conductor and return conductor—the half wave is 160 miles; the
complete wave therefore is $2 \times 160 = 320$ miles long, and
the duration of the wave is $\dfrac{320}{818,000} = \dfrac{1}{587}$ second, the
frequency 587 cycles, and if this short-circuit oscillation
extends into, and includes the generating system, the frequency may be still lower

Again, an oscillation of a very short section of the line, as
for instance, 100 feet $= \dfrac{100}{5280} = \dfrac{1}{52.8}$ mile wave length,
would have a duration of the wave of $\dfrac{1}{52.8 \times 188,000} =$
$\dfrac{1}{9,900,000}$ second, or a frequency of 9.9 millions of cycles per
second.

Hence the frequency of such oscillations, caused by the
readjustment of the stored energy of the system, may vary
from values below machine frequency, up to many millions of cycles per second. It is the higher, the shorter the
section of the circuit is in which the readjustment of energy
occurs. The higher the frequency, and therefore the shorter
the section of the circuit in which energy readjustment
occurs, obviously the less is the amount of energy which is
available in the oscillation—the stored energy of this section—and the less destructive therefore is the oscillation
That is, very high-frequency oscillations are of very low
energy and therefore of little destructiveness, but the energy
and thus the destructiveness of an oscillation increases with

decreasing frequency, and consequent increasing extent of the oscillation.

Such oscillations in a transmission line may result:

(*a*) From outside sources, atmospheric electric disturbances, as illustrated in the above instance.

(*b*) They occur during normal operation of the system· any change of load, or switching operation, as connecting or disconnecting circuits, etc., results in an oscillation, which usually is so small as to be harmless.

(*c*) It may result from a defect or fault in the circuit, as an arcing ground or spark discharge, etc.

One of the most serious and destructive oscillations or surges is that produced by a spark discharge to ground, or an arcing ground, in an overhead transmission line or an underground cable system.

Assuming for instance a 44,000-volt transmission line of 50 miles' length, which is insulated from ground, that is, in which the neutral is not grounded. At 44,000 volts between the line conductors, the voltage between each conductor and the ground, normally, that is, with all conductors insulated, is $\frac{44,000}{\sqrt{3}} = 25,000$. If now somewhere in the middle of this line an insulator breaks, and the conductor thus drops near the grounded insulator pin or cross arm to about 2 inches, with 25,000 volts between conductor and ground, a spark would jump from the conductor to the ground, at the broken insulator, over the 2-inch gap. This spark develops into an arc, over which the electrostatic charge of the conductor discharges to ground as current, and the voltage of this conductor against ground thus falls to zero, since it is grounded by the arc; the two other line conductors then have the full line voltage, of 44,000, against ground, and their electrostatic charge against ground therefore increases, from that corresponding to their normal potential of 25,000, to that corresponding to 44,000 volts. As soon as the first conductor has discharged and fallen to ground potential, the current from this conductor to ground, over the gap, ceases, the arc goes out, and the conductor so is again disconnected from ground   It then begins to charge again to its normal potential of 25,000 volts against ground, while the other two conductors discharge, from 44,000 down to 25,000 volts   As soon, however, as during the charge the voltage of the first conductor has risen to the voltage required to jump across a 2-inch gap, this conductor again discharges to ground by a spark, which develops into an arc and so on, the phenomena of discharge and charge of the conductor repeating continuously. Such an oscillation, which continues indefinitely, that is, until the defect in the circuit is remedied, or the circuit has broken down and gone out of service, is usually called a *surge.* The duration of each oscillation of such an arcing ground is the time required: (1) To develop the arc, (2) to discharge the line, (3) to extinguish the arc, (4) to charge the line   In the above instance, the time of charge or discharge of the 25 miles of line from the arcing ground to the terminal station is

$$\frac{25}{188,000} = \frac{1}{7250} \text{ second.}$$

Assuming the velocity of the arc stream as about 2000 feet per second, the development or extinction of a 2-inch arc would require

$$\frac{2}{12 \times 2000} = \frac{1}{12,000} \text{ second,}$$

and the total duration of one oscillation therefore is

$$\frac{1}{12,000} + \frac{1}{7520} + \frac{1}{12,000} + \frac{1}{7520} = \frac{1}{2300} \text{ second,}$$

so giving a frequency of 2300 cycles.

The two other lines therefore oscillate in voltage against ground, that is, charge and discharge also at a frequency of

2300 cycles. They receive their charge, however, over the transformers at the two ends of the line, and their capacity therefore is in series with the self-inductance of these transformers in the circuit of the surge frequency of 2300 cycles; and the voltage of the other two lines thus may build up by the combination of capacity and inductance in series, to excessive values; that is, a destructive breakdown occurs from the other lines to ground—or in the apparatus connected to them in the terminal stations of the line, as transformers, current transformers, etc.

A spark discharge or oscillating ground, therefore, is one of the most serious, as well as not infrequent disturbances on a long-distance transmission line or underground cable circuit, and it is mainly as a protection against this surge that it is recommended by many transmission engineers to ground the neutral of the system and so immediately convert a spark discharge on one conductor into a short-circuit of one phase of the system, and thereby automatically cut out the circuit; that is, rather shut down this circuit than continue operation with an arcing ground on the system. Where, as in underground cable systems, a number of cables are used in multiple, the immediate disconnection of an arcing cable undoubtedly is advisable.

As the overhead transmission line is immersed in the electric field of the atmosphere, any disturbance of the atmospheric electric field, whether by lightning between cloud and ground, or between or within clouds, thus must result in a disturbance and readjustment of the electrical condition of the transmission line. Thus a discharge between cloud and ground, in dropping the potential difference between cloud and ground, releases the bound electrostatic charge of the line, and thus causes a line discharge by what may be called electrostatic induction.

A lightning flash parallel to the line electromagnetically induces a line discharge, etc.; thus potential differences between line and ground occur by static induction from the atmospheric field, resulting in line discharges and currents flowing from the line, and currents are induced electromagnetically in the line by lightning flashes, etc., and produce potential differences and voltages in the line, usually of extremely abrupt character, that is, of very high frequency, where oscillating, reaching hundred thousands and millions of cycles per second.

In general such very high-frequency disturbances, or, more correctly speaking, very abrupt disturbances, as they are produced by atmospheric lightning as well as by circuit operation, as switching, may be divided into three classes:

(*a*) Impulses, that is, sudden waves of voltage or current, which are not oscillatory. They are perhaps the most common in transmission lines, are produced whenever a switch is closed or opened or any other change occurs. While non-oscillatory, we frequently denote their suddenness by a nominal or fictitious frequency, treating the impulse as half wave. Thus an impulse of 500 kilocycles would be an impulse in which the voltage rises at the same rate as it rises in a 500-kilocycle oscillation of the same maximum voltage

(*b*) Oscillations, that is, periodic disturbances which gradually die out, more or less rapidly, depending on the damping effect of the circuit resistance.

(*c*) Cumulative oscillations or surges, that is, oscillations which gradually increase in amplitude, until destruction of the circuit occurs, or they are finally limited by increasing energy losses.

The condenser discharge through an inductive circuit

may be oscillatory, or a single steady impulse of more or less steep wave front, depending on the resistance of the discharge circuit. With the transmission line, however, this is not the case, but in the same circuit, disturbances may be single impulses or may be oscillations, and both usually occur. Which takes place largely depends on the origin or cause of the disturbance

If the resistance of the circuit is very low, that is, the damping effect very small, and the circuit the set of an induced e.m.f., the oscillation may become cumulative, that is, increase in amplitude and build up to a stationary wave. It is obvious that such stationary waves or cumulative oscillations are the most destructive. Circuits, in which the resistance is sufficiently low, compared with the inductance and capacity, and therefore a material danger of the formation of stationary waves exists, are the high-potential windings of high-power transformers, and in these, cumulative oscillations have been observed and constitute indeed a serious source of danger. Somewhat less frequently, they also have been observed in the high-potential armature windings of large high-voltage alternators feeding directly into overhead lines.

EIGHTH LECTURE

GENERATION

For driving electric generators the following methods are available:

1. The hydraulic turbine in a water-power station.
2. The steam engine.
3. The steam turbine.
4. The gas engine.

COMPARISON OF PRIME MOVERS

1. The advantages of *water power, compared with steam power,* are:

(a) Very low cost of operation; no fuel, very little attendance

The disadvantages are

(a) Usually the cost of development and installation is far higher than with steam power.

(b) The location of the water power cannot be chosen freely, but is fixed by nature, therefore, the power cannot be used where generated, but a long-distance transmission line is required.

(c) Usually lower reliability of service, due to the dependence on a transmission line, and on meteorological conditions. the river may run dry in summer, ice interfere with the operation in winter.

The speed of the water in the turbine depends upon the head of water, and is approximately, in feet per minute, $480\sqrt{h}$, where h is the head, in feet. The peripheral speed of the turbine, and so its revolutions, depends upon the speed and therefore upon the head of the water. At high heads of 500 to 2000 feet, as are found in the West, the electric generators are thus high-speed machines, of good economy and moderate size and cost At low heads, however, such as are usual in the Eastern States, direct connection to a turbine leads to slow speed generators of many poles and large size and cost, while indirect driving, by belt or rope, is mechanically undesirable. Very low-head water powers of less than 20 to 30 feet head therefore usually are of little value and their development is economical only where very large power is available, or where electric power is valuable.

Of the two types of turbines, the reaction turbine runs approximately at the speed of the water, and the action or impulse turbine at half the speed of the water. At the same head and thus the same speed of the water, the reaction turbine gives higher speed, and is therefore used in water powers of low and medium heads, where the speed of the water is low; while the impulse turbine, as the Pelton wheel, is always used at very high heads, at which the reaction turbine would give too high speeds.

Where water power is not available, the power has to be generated by the combustion of fuel In this case, a greater freedom exists in the choice of the location of the plant; and it is located as near to the place of consumption as considerations of the cost of property, the availability of condensing water for the engines, the facilities of transportation, etc, permit Transmission lines, therefore, are less frequently used, but in steam stations of large power, high-potential distribution circuits of 6600, 11,000 or 22,000 volts, commonly underground by cables, are used in supplying electric power from the main generating

station, to the substations as centers of secondary distribution (New York, Chicago, etc)

As source of power is available then

The steam engine.   The steam turbine   The gas engine.

Comparison of the steam turbine with the steam engine·

Some of the advantages of the steam turbine over the
steam engine are

(*a*) High efficiency at low loads, and a flatter efficiency
curve, that is, the turbine efficiency remains high at partial
loads, and at overloads, where the steam engine efficiency
falls off greatly, so that the superiority of the steam turbine
in efficiency, while great at rated load, is still far greater at
partial load, light load and overload

(*b*) Smaller size, weight and space occupied.

(*c*) Uniform rate of rotation, therefore, decreased liability
of hunting of synchronous machines, and decreased necessity of heavy foundations to withstand reciprocating
strains.

(*d*) Greater reliability of operation and far less attendance required.

The steam turbine reaps a far greater benefit in economy
than the steam engine from superheat of the steam, and
from a high vacuum in the condenser

The disadvantage of the steam turbine is that in smaller
units, the superiority of the steam turbine over the steam
engine in efficiency, that is, in steam consumption, is less
marked, and when operating non-condensing, the simple
turbine offers little advantage in economy in small units.
Therefore, in units up to a few hundred horsepower, the
reciprocating steam engine still finds a large field in driving
electric generators, in isolated stations, etc , while for larger
units of thousands of kilowatt output, the reciprocating steam
engine has entirely been superseded by the steam turbine.

The speed characteristic of the steam turbine is similar to that of the constant-voltage direct-current shunt motor, or the polyphase induction motor; while that of the reciprocating steam engine is similar to that of the series motor. That is, to produce the same torque, the steam turbine requires approximately the same amount of steam, irrespective of the speed, therefore, its efficiency is highest at a certain speed, or rather range of speed, but falls off with the speed, while the steam consumption of the reciprocating engine, at constant torque, is approximately proportional to the speed, that is the number of times the cylinders are filled per minute. Or in other words, the torque per pound of steam used per minute is approximately constant and independent of the speed in the turbine (just as the torque per volt-ampere is approximately constant for all speeds in the induction motor), while in the reciprocating engine the torque per pound of steam used per minute is approximately inversely proportional to the speed, or at least greatly increases with decrease of speed (just as in the series motor the torque per volt-ampere input increases with decrease of speed)

The steam turbine, therefore, would not be suitable for directly driving a railway train in rapid transit service, but is suitable for driving the ship's propeller.

Just as in the induction motor a series of economical speeds can be produced by changing the number of poles, so in the steam turbine a series of economical speeds can be produced by changing the number of expansions. For driving electrical machinery this, however, is of no importance.

Comparison of the gas engine with the steam turbine and the steam engine

The leading and foremost advantage of the gas engine,

and the feature which gives it the right of existence, is its high efficiency. That is, the same amount of coal, converted to gas and fed to a good gas engine, gives more power than when burned under the boilers of the engine, except perhaps the very large and exceedingly efficient steam-turbine units. The cause is that the gas engine works over a far greater temperature range than the steam engine and even the steam turbine—although the latter, by its ability to economically utilize superheat and high condenser vacuum, gets the benefit of a larger temperature range over the steam engine.

If, therefore, the gas engine were not so very greatly handicapped in every other respect, it would long have superseded the steam engine and even the steam turbine, except perhaps in the largest sizes.

The disadvantages of the gas engine in every respect but efficiency are such, however, that in spite of its existence of over half a century it has not made a serious impression on the industry; while the steam turbine during the short time of its existence has entirely replaced the steam engine in large electric generating plants.

The cause of the disadvantages of the gas engine is the high maximum temperature and the high maximum pressure compared with the mean pressure in the cylinders, which is necessary to get the greater temperature range and thus the efficiency, therefore, is inherent in this type of apparatus.

The output depends upon the mean pressure in the cylinder, which is relatively low, the strains on the maximum pressure, which is very high; and the gas engine, therefore, must be very large, and its moving parts very strong and heavy, for its output. The impulse due to the rapid pressure change is very jerky—almost of the nature of an explosion—and the steadiness of the rate of rotation is, therefore, very low, requiring for electric driving very heavy flywheels and numerous cylinders

Compared with the steam engine, the disadvantages of the gas engine so are:

(*a*) Lower reliability; higher cost of maintenance in attendance, repairs, and greater depreciation

(*b*) Larger size and space occupation for the same output

(*c*) Less easy to start.

(*d*) In general, lower steadiness of the rate of rotation

The advantage of the gas engine is, that it requires no boiler plant; the compensating disadvantage, that it requires a gas-generating plant. This latter disadvantage disappears where gas is available as fuel—in the waste gases of blast furnaces of steel plants and in the natural gas districts—and in those cases gas engines have found their introduction. They have also been installed for smaller powers, where low cost of fuel is unessential, but the operation of a steam boiler is objectionable, as in isolated plants using city gas or liquid fuel (gasolene, etc.).

In general, however, with the exception of those special cases, the gas engine does not yet come into consideration in the electric-power generating station

ELECTRIC GENERATORS

In general, considerations of economy make it desirable to generate the electric power in the form in which it is used In most cases, however, this is not feasible, but a higher voltage or even a different form of power (alternating instead of direct) is necessary in the generating station than that required by the user, to enable transmission and distribution, and then usually three-phase alternating current is generated.

1. For isolated plants, and in general distribution of such small extent as to be within range of 220-volt distribution, 220-volt direct-current generators are used, operating a three-wire system, formerly two 110-volt machines, supplying the two sides of the system, now almost always 200-volt machines, deriving the neutral by equalizer machines, or by connection to a storage battery, or by compensator and collector rings on the 220-volt generator. That is, two diametrically opposite (electrically) points of the armature winding are connected to collector rings (so giving

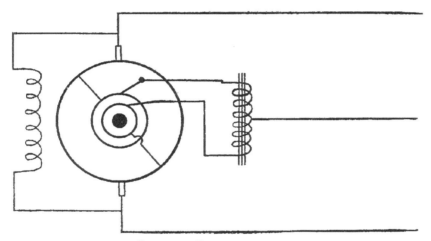

Fig. 24.—Three-wire generator.

an alternating-current voltage on those collector rings), an alternating-current auto-transformer (transformer with a single winding) is connected between the collector rings, and the neutral brought out from the center of the auto-transformer, as shown diagrammatically in Fig. 24. This arrangement is now most commonly used.

For direct-current distribution in larger cities, such generating stations have practically disappeared, and have been replaced by converter substations, receiving power from a main generating station, as three-phase alternating

current of 6600, 11,000 or 20,000 volts, and 25 or 60
cycles. They are used, however, very largely for isolated
plants, in large office buildings, apartment houses, etc

2. For street railway, 600-volt direct-current generators
are still used to some extent, where the railway system is
of moderate extent. In large railway systems, and roads
covering greater distances, as interurban trolley lines,
direct generation of 600 volts direct current has practically
disappeared before the railway converter substation, receiving power as three-phase alternating from transmission lines or high-voltage distribution cables

3. For general distribution by alternating current, with
a 2200-volt primary system, direct generation is still to a
considerable extent used, often by a four-wire primary
system (page 32, §4), as the use of 2200-volt permits the
system to cover a very large territory, and substations are
mainly used only where the power can be derived from a
long-distance transmission line, or where the 2200-volt
distribution is only a part of a large system of electric
generation, as in the suburban distribution of large cities,
using converter substations for the interior. In this case,
where the transmission line or the main generating station
is at 60 cycles, large station transformers are used for the
supply of the 2200-volt distribution, where the power
supply is at 25 cycles, either frequency converters, or
motor generators change to 60 cycles, 2200 volts

4. For special use, as for electrochemical work, where the
electric power is generated directly, different voltages, etc ,
may be used to suit the requirements.

Where the power cannot be generated in the form in
which it is used, and that is the case in all larger systems,
three-phase alternators are almost universally used.

The single-phase system has the disadvantage that

single-phase induction and synchronous motors and converters are inferior to polyphase machines, and single-phase alternators larger and less efficient, and for lighting, where single-phase is preferable, single-phase lighting circuits can be operated from polyphase alternators.

It must be considered that in the modern large generating system, the lighting load often is only a small part of the total load.

Two-phase also has practically gone out of use, since it offers no advantage over the three-phase, and the three-phase is preferable for transmission, requiring only three conductors, while two-phase requires four.

In polyphase alternators the flow of power is constant, that is, at any moment adding the power of all phases gives the same value, while in single-phase alternators the power is pulsating

In a polyphase machine the armature reaction also is constant, in a single-phase machine, pulsating; in the latter therefore, in machines of very large armature reaction, as turbo-alternators, pulsations of the magnet field, and thereby loss in efficiency, and heating may result.

An alternator has armature reaction and self-induction.

The armature reaction is the magnetic action of the armature current on the field, that is, the armature current demagnetizes or magnetizes the field according to its phase, and so lowers or raises the voltage. Armature reaction, therefore, is expressed in ampere-turns.

Self-induction is the action of the armature current in producing magnetism in the armature, which magnetism does not go through the field. This magnetism induces an e m f in the armature, which opposes or assists the e m f produced by the field magnetism, according to the phase of the armature current, and so lowers or raises the voltage.

Self-induction, or "armature *reactance*" therefore is expressed in ohms

Armature reaction and self-induction therefore act in the same manner, lowering the voltage with lagging and raising the voltage with leading current

In calculating alternators, either the armature reaction and the self-induction can both be considered, which makes the calculation more complicated, or the armature reaction may be neglected and the self-induction made so much larger as to allow for the armature reaction. This self-induction is then called the "synchronous reactance" and, combined with the armature resistance, the "synchronous impedance" of the machine. Or the self-induction may be neglected and only the armature reaction considered, but which is increased to allow for the self-induction.

The last way (armature reaction), is used in designing machines, the second way (synchronous reactance) in calculations with machines and systems

In the momentary short-circuit current of alternators, however, the armature reaction and the self-induction must be considered separately, since they act differently.

In the moment of short-circuiting an alternator, the self-induction acts immediately in limiting the current, but not so the armature reaction, because it takes time before the armature current demagnetizes the field, that is, the field exciting winding acts as a short-circuited secondary around the field poles, and retards the decrease of field magnetism resulting from the demagnetizing action of the armature current by inducing a current in the field winding, which tends to maintain the field magnetism.

Therefore, in the first moment after the short-circuit the armature current is limited by self-induction only, and

7

is therefore much larger than afterwards, when self-induction and armature reaction both act.

In machines of low armature reaction and high self-induction, as high-frequency alternators, the momentary short-circuit current is not much larger than the permanent short-circuit current. In machines of low self-induction, that is, of a well-distributed armature winding, but high armature reaction, (that is, very large output per pole, as in steam turbine alternators), the momentary short-circuit current may be many times greater than the permanent value of the short-circuit current, which is reached after a few seconds.

In the moment of short-circuiting such an alternator, the field current rises to several times its normal value, and becomes pulsating Gradually the armature current and the field current die down to their normal values.

Since the regulation of such alternators mainly depends upon the armature reaction, which is very large compared with the self-induction, even a considerable external self-induction inserted as reactive coil for limiting the momentary short-circuit current does not much increase the combined effect of armature reaction and self-induction; that is, does not seriously affect the regulation, and besides, in very large systems, the regulation of the generators is immaterial

In large steam-turbine alternators, the momentary short-circuit current may reach 20 to 30 times full-load current, and in large generating stations, having a number of such turbo-alternators feeding into the busbars, a short-circuit at or near the busbars thus may cause momentarily currents to flow, amounting to several million kilovolt-amperes, and therefore extremely destructive by their energy, in circuit-breakers, etc , and destructive by the mechanical magnetic forces in machines, transformers, etc. It therefore becomes necessary and has become the practice in such large high-power systems, to limit the momentary short-circuit currents by inserting power limiting reactances into the generator leads, and in very large systems also in the feeder circuits, and to divide the busbars into sections by busbar reactances. Such power-limiting reactances must be built so as not to saturate magnetically even at short-circuit current, and therefore are built without iron, that is, with air cores.

NINTH LECTURE

HUNTING OF SYNCHRONOUS MACHINES

Cross-currents can flow between alternators due to differences in voltage, that is, differences in excitation; and due to differences in phase, that is, differences in position of their rotors.

Cross-currents due to differences in excitation are wattless currents, magnetizing the underexcited and demagnetizing the overexcited machine

Cross-currents due to differences in position are energy currents, accelerating the lagging and retarding the leading machine   Their magnetic action is a distortion or a shift of the field, that is, they increase the magnetic density at the one and decrease it at the other pole corner.

If two machines are thrown together out of phase, or brought out of the phase by some cause (as the beat of an engine, or the change of load of a synchronous motor) then the two machines pull each other in phase again, oscillate a few times against each other, which oscillation gradually decreases and dies out, and the machines run steadily.

If the oscillations do not decrease, but continue, the machines are said to be hunting.

If the oscillation is small it may do no harm; if it is greater, it may cause fluctuation of voltage, resulting in flickering of lights, etc.; if it gets very large, it may throw the machines out of step.

Some causes of hunting are:

First.—Magnetic lag.

Second.—Pulsation of engine speed.

Third—Hunting of engine governors

Fourth.—Wrong speed characteristic of engine.

First.—When the machines move apart from each other, magnetic attraction opposes their separation. When they pull together again, magnetic attraction pushes them together with the same force, so that they would move over the position of coincidence in phase and separate again in the opposite direction just as much as before

Energy losses as friction, etc , retard the separation and so make them separate less than before, every time they do so, that is, cause them gradually to stop seesawing

If, however, there is a lag in the magnetic attraction, then they come together with greater force than they separated, so separate more in the opposite direction, that is, the oscillation increases until the machines fall out of step, or the further increase of oscillation is stopped by the increasing energy losses.

This kind of hunting is stopped by increasing the energy losses due to the oscillation, by copper bridges between the poles, by aluminum collars around the pole faces, or most effectively by a complete squirrel-cage winding in the pole faces.

The frequency of this hunting depends on the magnetic attraction, that is, on the field excitation, and on the weight of the rotating mass The higher the field excitation the greater is the magnetic force, that is, quicker the motion of the machine and therefore the higher the frequency. The greater the weight, the slower it is set in motion, that is, the lower the frequency.

Characteristic of this hunting therefore is that its frequency is changed by changing the field excitation.

Second.—If the speed of the engine varies during the rotation, rising and falling with the steam impulses, then the alternator speed and the frequency also pulsate with a speed equal to, or a multiple of the engine speed. If now two such alternators happen to be thrown together so that the moment of maximum frequency of one coincides with the moment of minimum frequency of the other, the two machines cannot run in perfect phase with each other, but pulsate, alternatingly getting out of phase with each other, coming together, and getting out again in the opposite direction   If the deviation of the two engines from uniform rate of rotation is very little—the maximum displacement of the alternator from the position of uniform rotation not more than three electrical degrees—the pulsating cross-currents, which flow between the alternators, are moderate, and the phenomenon harmless, as long as the oscillation is not cumulative. An increase of the weight of the flywheel of the engine decreases the speed pulsation and thereby decreases this form of hunting, which is the most harmless, but increases the tendency to the hunting in No. 1 and No. 3, and therefore is not desirable, but steadiness of engine speed should be secured by the design of the engine, that is, by balancing the different forces in the engine, as the steam impulses and the momentum of the reciprocating masses, so as to give a uniform resultant.

In such a case, when running from a single alternator, driven by a reciprocating engine with moderate speed pulsation (therefore receiving a slightly pulsating frequency), a synchronous motor without anti-hunting devices, but of high armature reaction, and therefore high stability, may run very steadily, with no appreciable current pulsation, while the same synchronous motor, when supplied with a squirrel-cage winding in the field pole faces as the most powerful anti-hunting device, may show pulsation in the current supplied, which in a high-speed motor, of high momentum, may be considerable. The cause is, that in the former case the synchronous motor does not follow the pulsation of frequency, but keeps constant speed, while in the latter case the squirrel-cage winding forces the motor to follow the variation in frequency by accelerating and decelerating, and the pulsation of the current therefore is not hunting, but energy current required to make the motor speed follow the engine pulsation.

If the frequency of oscillation of the machine (as determined by its field excitation and the weight of its moving part) is the same as the frequency of engine impulses, that is, the same as the number of engine revolutions or a multiple thereof, then successive engine impulses will always come at the same moment of the machine beat and so continuously increase it   that is, the machine oscillation increases, or the machine hunts.

In this case of cumulative hunting caused by the engine impulses, the frequency of oscillation agrees' with the engine oscillation.

Third.—If one alternator is a little ahead, that is, takes a little more load, its engine governor regulates by reducing the steam, slowing down the alternator to its normal position. When slowing down, the flywheel is giving power, therefore the steam supply has been reduced more than it should be, that is, the alternator drops behind and takes less load until the governor has admitted steam again.

In the meantime, while the first alternator was behind and took less load, the second alternator had to take the load, that is, the governor of the second alternator admitted more steam. When the first alternator has picked up again to its normal load, the second alternator gets too much steam and its governor must cut off, but then cuts off too much, the same way as the first alternator did before; so the two governors hunt against each other by alternatingly admitting too much and too little steam.

In this case the frequency of hunting does not depend on the engine speed and does not vary much with the field excitation, but the hunting is usually much less at heavy load than at light load. The reason is that at load, when the engines take much steam, a little change in the steam supply does not make so much difference as at light load, where the engines take very little steam, and so a small change of the governor has a great effect.

Fourth —To run in parallel, the speed of the engines driving the alternators must decrease with the load so that the alternators divide the load

If the speed did not change with the load, then there would be no division of the load; the one engine could take all the load, the other nothing

If the speed curve of the engine is such that the speed does not fall off much between no load and moderate load, then the alternators will not well divide the load at light loads, and hunt while running in parallel at light load, but steady down at heavier loads.

To distinguish between different kinds of hunting:

First.—Change of frequency with change of field excitation points to magnetic hunting, especially if very marked.

Second.—Equality of frequency with the generator speed points to engine hunting

Third —If the synchronous motor or converter steadies down when only one engine is running, it points to engine governor hunting

Fourth —Steadiness of operation at load, and unsteadiness at light load points to governor hunting, but may also be due to engine and magnetic hunting.

Fifth—If by disconnecting one governor and governing one engine only, the hunting disappears, then it is due to governor hunting. If it does not disappear, then both governors may be disconnected and the engines run carefully without governors, by throttle. If the hunting then disappears, it is due to the governors, if it does not disappear, it is probably magnetic hunting.

If by making the field excitation of the two alternators or two converters that hunt, unequal—by increasing the one and decreasing the other—the hunting disappears or decreases, it is magnetic hunting.

In a case of hunting, the following points should be investigated:

A. HUNTING OF SYNCHRONOUS MOTORS OR CONVERTERS

First.—Count the number of beats to get the frequency of hunting. If the beats periodically increase and decrease, it shows two frequencies of hunting superimposed upon each other. Then count the total number of beats per minute (counting during intermissions) and count the number of intermissions per minute.

The two frequencies are the number of beats per minute, plus and minus half the number of intermissions or nodes per minute.

Instance: 80 beats per minute, 10 intermissions per minute. Frequencies $80 + 5$ and $80 - 5$ or 85 and 75 beats.

If one of the two frequencies approximately coincides with the engine speed, it can be assumed as the engine speed. The number of revolutions of the engine obviously should be counted also.

Second—See whether any machine in the system runs at a speed equal to the observed frequency of hunting.

For instance, a generator may make 75 revolutions per minute, which accounts for this frequency

Third —With several converters in the same station see whether the station ammeter also hunts.

If the station ammeter is very steady and the converter ammeters hunt, the converters hunt against each other. In this case lowering the one and raising the other converter field and, if necessary, readjusting the potential regulators, may stop the hunting by giving the two machines different frequencies of hunting which interfere with each other

If all three meters are unsteady, the converters may hunt against each other or hunt together against another station or against the generator. Then find out whether the ammeter needles of both converters go up and down together or one goes up when the other goes down.

Fourth —Change the field excitation and see whether the change of field excitation changes the frequency. See whether a decrease of field excitation steadies it Occasionally hunting can be stopped by lowering the field excitation, that is, running with lagging current.

Fifth —If several converters of a substation feed into the same direct-current system, as the converters of other substations, disconnect the direct-current sides of the converters and see if they still hunt.

If two or more converters run in the same station, run only one and see whether it hunts

Cure.—*First.*—If the hunting is magnetic hunting between converters or synchronous motors, it is frequently reduced by making the field excitation unequal, or putting a flywheel on one converter, or belting some other machine to it, or running an induction motor in the same station or in any other way breaking up the resonance.

Second —Several converters hunting against each other in the same substation are frequently steadied by connecting the collector rings with each other, that is, by equalizer connections between converter and transformer or regulator.

In this case the commutator brushes have to be carefully adjusted to avoid sparking

Third.—The most effective way is to put copper bridges on the converters or synchronous motors, or better still a squirrel-cage winding in the field pole faces.

Not so good are short-circuiting rings around the field poles

B. HUNTING OF GENERATORS

First —Count the frequency in the same way as before.

Second —See whether the frequency agrees with the generator speed or with the speed of some large motor on the system.

Third —See whether the frequency changes with the excitation.

Fourth —See whether the hunting changes with the load, that is, gets worse at light load.

Fifth.—Disconnect governors and see whether this stops hunting.

Cure.—*First.*—If the hunting stops when disconnecting the governors, it is hunting of the governors and can be cured by putting a stiff dashpot on the governors

Second —If the hunting does not stop by disconnecting the governors, copper bridges on the alternators will cure it.

Third.—If the hunting has the speed of the engine, it may be reduced by increasing the flywheel or decreasing it, by running an induction motor in the station, or in any other way breaking up the resonance.

In general, systems having all kinds of loads, different sizes of generators, motors and converters, induction motors and synchronous motors mixed, etc., are very little liable to hunting Hunting is most liable to occur when all the generators are of the same kind and all the synchronous motors or converters are of the same kind.

Resistance in general increases the tendency to hunting so that if the resistance drop is more than 10 to 15 per cent , special precautions have to be taken, such as squirrel-cage pole-face windings, or synchronous machines must be altogether avoided and induction motor-generator sets used.

Reactance between the machines decreases the tendency except when very large

The tendency to hunting is more severe at the end of long-distance transmission lines and induction machines are therefore often preferable in such a place or synchronous machines with squirrel-cage pole-face winding.

Machines with high armature reaction are much less liable to hunt than machines with low armature reaction, that is, close regulation, because with high armature reaction the current varies much less with a change of position of the machine. Therefore, 60-cycle converters are more liable to hunt than 25-cycle converters, because in 60-cycle converters there is not so much space on the armature to get high armature reaction.

TENTH LECTURE

REGULATION AND CONTROL

A. DIRECT-CURRENT SYSTEMS

In *direct-current three-wire 220-volt distribution systems* several outside busbars are used and, with change of load, the feeders are changed from one busbar to another.

The different busbars are connected to different machines, to the storage battery or to boosters

The lighting boosters are low-voltage machines separately excited from the busbars   The main generators are shunt machines or rather are excited from the busbars, or rotary converters, and are usually of 250 volts, that is, the neutral brought out by collector rings and compensator.

In railway circuits, in addition to trolley wire and rail return, trolley feeders and ground feeders, or plus and minus feeders are sufficient for converter substations, and where the distance gets too great for feeders, another substation is installed.

When using direct-current generators, series boosters are used to feed very long feeders which otherwise would have an excessive drop of voltage.   In this way feeder drops of 200 to 300 volts are taken care of by the railway booster. Such a large voltage drop is uneconomical and railway boosters are therefore used only for small sections for which it does not pay to install a separate station, especially where the load is very temporary, as for instance, heavy Sunday load, etc.

Railway boosters are series machines, that is, the series field and the machine voltage therefore are proportional

109

to the current. In such railway boosters it is necessary to take care in the booster design that it does not build up as series generator feeding a current through the local circuit between a short feeder and a long feeder, as shown in Fig. 25.

A series machine excites if the resistance of its circuit is less than a certain critical value. To avoid such local circuit, either the trolley circuit is cut between the feeders, or the boosting kept below the critical value.

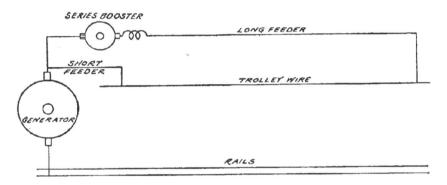

FIG. 25.—Series railway booster.

This feature of building up and short-circuiting, if the resistance of the circuit is too low, is characteristic of all series boosters, and to be looked out for.

If the distances are too great for boosters, inverted converters in the generating station are used to change from direct current to alternating current; the alternating current is sent by step-up and step-down transformers to the substation and changed to direct current by rotary converters.

If a considerable amount of power is required at a distance, it is more convenient at the generating station to use, instead of inverted converters, double current generators, that is, generators having commutator and collector rings.

If most of the power is used at a distance, alternating-current generators are used with rotary converters and frequently one converter substation is located in the generating station.

Inverted converters and double current generators are now used very little, since usually the systems are now so large as to require most of the power at a distance, and therefore alternating-current generators are used.

Many big systems have advanced from direct-current generators, through inverted converters and double current generators, to the present alternators feeding converter substations.

B. LOCAL ALTERNATING-CURRENT SYSTEMS

Generator Regulation.—*First.*—Close inherent regulation   .

This is secured by low armature reaction and high saturation so that the voltage does not vary much with the load.

Advantages—

Simple, requiring no additional apparatus, etc

Instantaneous.

Disadvantages—

Larger and more expensive generators and when of very close regulation, more difficult to run in parallel

Second —Rectifying Commutator

The main current goes over a commutator, is rectified, and the rectified current sent through a series field.   This arrangement is not used any more

Advantage—

Permits compounding and overcompounding without any elaborate apparatus.

Disadvantages—

Only limited power can be rectified, therefore suitable only for smaller machines.

Compounds correctly only for constant power factor; that is, if compounded for non-inductive load, the voltage drops on inductive load, since inductive load requires a greater field excitation than non-inductive load.

Brushes have to be shifted with change of power factor, that is, change from motor load to lighting load, etc.; otherwise commutator sparks badly.

These machines therefore were good in the early days when all the load was lighting load, but are unsuited at present for mixed load.

Third —Potential Regulator.

Tirrill Regulator.—Rheostat in exciter field so large that when in circuit the excitation is the lowest, and that when short-circuited the excitation is the highest ever required.

A potential magnet in the alternator circuit operates a contact-maker which continuously cuts the resistance in and out again, so that the contact-maker is never at rest, but always cuts in and out, and the average field excitation of the exciter is between maximum and minimum.

If the voltage tends to drop, the contact remains a shorter time on the low than on the high position, and so raises excitation; if the voltage tends to rise, the contact-maker remains a shorter time on the high than on the low position, and so lowers excitation.

Advantages—

Very simple.

Can be applied to any alternator and requires no special readjustment.

Disadvantages—

Additional device which requires some attention and adjustment.

In very large machines often no regulating device is used but hand control of the field rheostat, since in such large machines the load only varies slowly and never changes much, as for reasons of economy the machines are run full load; with the change of load, machines are shut down or started up.

Synchronous Motors and Converters.

In an alternating-current system or part of the system containing large synchronous motors or converters the voltage can be controlled by varying the motor or converter field in the same way as with alternators, that is, by Tirrill regulator or commutator and series field, etc.

Potential Regulators.

(*a*) Compensator regulator.

With step-up or step-down transformers the voltage can be regulated by having different taps brought out of the transformer winding and so get different voltages by means of a dial switch. Where no transformers are used an auto-transformer with different voltage taps gives the same results.

The taps can be brought out in the primary or in the secondary, whichever is the most convenient: in the secondary, if the primary is of very high voltage; in the primary, if the secondary is of very low voltage and large current

Advantages—

Simplest, cheapest and most efficient

Disadvantages—

Step-by-step variation.

(*b*) Induction regulator.

Built like induction motors with stationary primary in shunt and movable secondary in series to the line.

By moving the secondary the voltage varies from lowering to raising.

8

Induction regulators are usually three-phase and of larger sizes for rotary converters in lighting systems.

When single-phase, the stationary member contains a short-circuited coil at right angles to the primary. In the neutral position this coil acts as short-circuited secondary to the secondary coil, and so reduces its self-induction.

Advantages—

Perfectly uniform variation and considerable inductance which is of advantage for rotary converters.

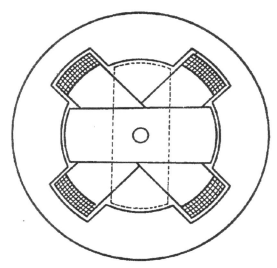

Fig. 26.—Magneto regulator.

Disadvantages—

High cost.

(*c*) Magneto regulator.

A stationary primary coil is in shunt and a stationary secondary coil is in series and at right angles to the primary; an iron shuttle moves inside of the coils and so turns the magnetism of the primary coil into the secondary coil either one way or the other.

On the dotted position the primary sends the magnetism

through the secondary in opposite direction as in the drawn position, in Fig. 26.

Advantage—

Uniform variation

Disadvantage—

More expensive than compensator regulator.

C. GENERAL POWER-GENERATING SYSTEMS

With the advances of electrical engineering, electric power generation for all purposes, lighting, domestic and industrial power, railroading, etc , is more and more being centralized in huge three-phase high-voltage steam-turbine stations, often interconnected with hydraulic stations. In these vast stations, of total capacities of hundred thousands of kilowatts connected to the busbars, the regulation of the generators has ceased to be of any moment in the voltage control, as the greatest sudden change of load, which may normally be expected, is too small to affect the busbar voltage of such a system.

The generators thus are usually operated with exciters controlled by Tirrill regulators for constant voltage, and the serious problem of such systems is not the voltage regulation, but is the power limitation, is to reduce the amount of power, which in case of accident can be let loose at any point of the system, to a value which can be controlled without serious danger of self-destruction of the system. The solution hereof has been found in the extensive use of reactances in the generator leads, in the busbars and often in the feeders, together with a generator design securing the highest possible internal reactance That is, in this case, not the close regulation of low reactance, as desired in the small isolated generators of old, is aimed at, but the reverse is made necessary by the safety of the system: high reactance and limitation of the power.

ELEVENTH LECTURE

LIGHTNING PROTECTION

When the first telegraph circuits were strung across the country, lightning protection became necessary, and was given to these circuits at the station by connecting spark gaps between the circuit conductors and the ground.

When, however, electric light and power circuits made their appearance, this protection against lightning by a simple small spark gap to ground became insufficient, and this additional problem arose to open the short-circuit of the machine current, which resulted from and followed the lightning discharge

This problem of opening the circuit after the discharge was solved by the magnetic blowout, which is still used to a large extent on 500-volt railway circuits; by the horn gap arrester—a gap between two horn-shaped terminals, between which the arc rises, and so lengthens itself until it blows out; and later on, for alternating current, the multigap between non-arcing metal cylinders, a number of small spark gaps in series with each other, between line and ground, over which the lightning discharges to ground— the machine current following as arc, but stopped at the end of the half wave of alternating current, and not starting at the next half wave, due to the property of these "non-arcing" metals (usually zinc-copper alloys), to carry an arc in one direction, but requiring an extremely high voltage to start a reverse arc.

These lightning arresters operated satisfactorily with the smaller machines and circuits of limited power used in the earlier days, but when large machines of close regulation, and therefore of very large momentary overload capacity were introduced, and a number of such machines operated in multiple, these lightning arresters became insufficient the machine current following the lightning discharge frequently was so enormous that the circuit did not open at the end of the half wave, but the arrester held an arc and burned up.

Furthermore, the introduction of synchronous motors, and of parallel operation of generators, made it essential that the lightning arrester should open again instantly after discharge For, if the short-circuit current over the arrester lasted for any appreciable time: a few seconds, synchronous motors and converters dropped out of step, the generators broke their synchronism, and the system in this way would be shut down. The horn gap arrester, in which the arc rises between horn-shaped terminals, and by lengthening, blows itself out, therefore became unsuitable for general service, since without series resistance, the short-circuiting arc lasted too long for synchronous apparatus to remain in step, and with series resistance reducing the current so as not to affect synchronous machines, it failed to protect under severe conditions Thus it has been relegated for use as an emergency arrester on some overhead lines, to operate only when a shutdown is unavoidable, and as auxiliary to other arresters

To limit the machine current which followed the lightning discharge, and so enable the lightning arrester to open the discharge circuit, series resistance was introduced in the arrester. Series resistance, however, also limited the discharge current, and with very heavy discharges, such lightning arresters with series resistance failed to protect the circuits, that is, failed to discharge the abnormal voltage without destructive pressure rise. This difficulty was solved by the introduction of shunted resistances, that is, resistances shunting a part of the spark gaps All the minor discharges then pass over the resistances and the unshunted spark gaps, the resistance assisting in opening the machine circuit after the discharge Very heavy discharges pass over all the spark gaps, as a path without resistance, but those spark gaps which are shunted by the resistance, open after the discharge, the machine current, after the first discharge, therefore is deflected over the resistances, limited thereby, and the circuit so finally opened by the unshunted spark gaps.

With the change in the character, size and power of electric circuits, the problem of their protection against lightning thus also changed and became far more serious and difficult Other forms of lightning, which did not exist in the small electric circuits of early days, also made their appearance, and protection now is required not only against the damage threatened by atmospheric lightning, but also against "lightning" originating in the circuits· so called "internal lightning," which is frequently far more dangerous than the disturbances caused by thunder storms.

Under lightning in its broadest sense we now understand all the phenomena of electric power when beyond control.

Electric power, when getting beyond control may mean excessive currents, or excessive voltages, or excessive suddenness high frequency and steep wave fronts of impulses. Excessive currents are usually of serious moment only in systems of very high power since the damage done by excessive currents is usually due to heating, and even very excessive currents require an appreciable time before producing dangerous temperatures, usually circuit-breakers, automatic cutouts, etc., can take care of excessive currents, and such currents produce damage only in those instances where they occur at the moment of opening or closing a switch, by burning contacts, or where the mechanical forces exerted by them are dangerously large, as with the short-circuit currents of the modern huge turbo-generators, and in general in systems of high power concentration.

Excessive voltage is practically instantaneous in its action, and the problem of lightning protection therefore is essentially that of protecting against excessive voltages.

The performance of the lightning arrester on an electric circuit is analogous to that of the safety valve on the steam boiler, that is, to protect against dangerous pressures—whether steam pressure or electric pressure—by opening a discharge path as soon as the pressure approaches the danger limit. Therefore absolute reliability is required in its operation, and discharge with as little shock as possible, but over a path amply large to discharge practically unlimited power without dangerous pressure rise.

However, the causes of excessive pressures, and the forms which such pressures may assume, are so much more varied in electric circuits than with steam pressures, that the design of perfectly satisfactory lightning arresters has been a far more difficult problem than the design of the steam safety valve.

Such excessive pressures may enter the electric circuit from the outside by atmospheric disturbances as lightning, or may originate in the circuit

Excessive pressures in electric circuits may be single peaks of pressure, or "strokes" or discharges, or multiple strokes, that is, several strokes following each other in rapid succession, with intervals from a small fraction of a second to a few seconds, or such excessive pressures may be practically continuous, the strokes following each other in rapid succession, thousands per second, sometimes for hours.

Atmospheric disturbances, as cloud lightning, usually give single strokes, but quite frequently multiple strokes, as has been shown by the oscillograms secured of such lightning discharges from transmission lines Any lightning arrester to protect the system must therefore be operative again immediately after the discharge, since very often a second and a third discharge follows immediately after the discharge within a second or less

Continuous discharges, or recurrent surges (lightning lasting continuously for long periods of time with thousands of high-voltage peaks per second), mainly originate in the circuits by an arcing ground, spark discharge over broken insulators, faults in cables, etc. However, this fault in the circuit frequently is caused by a lightning discharge, for instance by a flashing over of an insulator, so that lightning may be the ultimate cause of the surge.   These phenomena, which have made their appearance only with the development of the modern high-power high-voltage electric systems, become of increasing severity and danger with the increase in size and power of electric systems.

Single strokes and multiple strokes, that is, all the disturbances directly due to atmospheric electricity, as cloud lightning, are safely taken care of by the modern multi-gap lightning arrester. In its usual form for high alternating voltages, it comprises a large number of spark gaps, connected between line and ground, and shunted by resistances of different sizes, as shown in Fig. 27, in such manner that a high pressure discharge of very low quantity, as the gradual accumulation of static charge on the system, discharges over a path of very high resistance R_1, and so

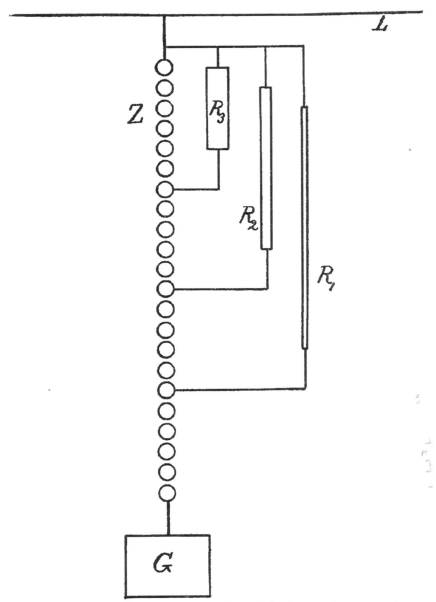

FIG. 27—High-voltage multi-gap lightning arrester.

discharges inappreciably and even frequently invisibly.
A disturbance of somewhat higher power finds a discharge
path of moderate resistance R_2, and so discharges with
moderate current, that is, without shock on the system;
while a high power disturbance finds a discharge path

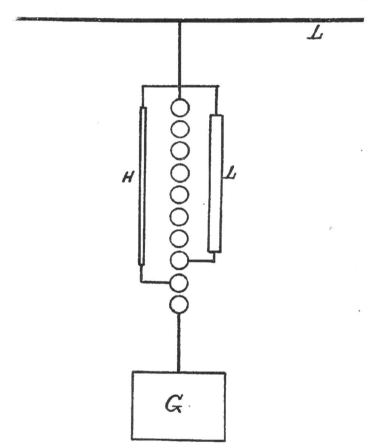

FIG. 28.—Multi-gap lightning arrester.

over a low resistance R_3, and, if of very great power, even
over a path of zero resistance, Z. On medium voltage,
commonly only two resistances are used, one high and one
moderately low, as shown by the diagram of a 2000-volt
multi-gap arrester, Fig. 28, and on voltages of 2300 to

10,000, commonly a single resistance is used, which is partly in shunt, partly in series to the gaps. Gaps and resistance are enclosed in a closed tube, so as to get the assistance of the pressure created by the discharge, for opening the circuit. This type of the arrester, therefore, is called the Compression Chamber Arrester. It is generally used for primary alternating-current distribution circuits, and, as stated, is a type of multi-gap arrester.

The resistance of the discharge path of the present multi-gap arrester therefore is approximately inversely proportional to the volume of the discharge. This is an essential and important feature Occasionally discharges of such large volume occur, as to require a discharge path of no resistance, as any resistance would not allow a sufficient discharge to keep the voltage within safe limits. At the same time the discharge should not occur over a path without a resistance or of very low resistance, except when necessary, since the momentary short-circuit—that is, the short-circuit for a part of the half wave—of a resistanceless discharge is a severe shock on the system, which must be avoided wherever permissible.

This type of lightning arrester takes care of single discharges and of multiple discharges, no matter how frequently they occur or how rapidly they follow each other, with the minimum possible shock on the system. It cannot take care, however, of continuous lightning—those disturbances, mainly originating in the system, where the voltage remains excessive continuously (or rather rises thousands of times per second to excessive values), and for long times. With such a recurring surge, the multi-gap arrester would discharge continuously in protecting the system, until it destroys itself by the excessive power of the continuously succeeding discharges.

Where such continuous lightning may occur frequently, as in large high-power systems, and in all high-voltage transmission lines, due to the line capacity, and the system requires protection against them, a type of lightning arrester which can discharge continuously, at least for a considerable time, without self-destruction, is necessary. The lightning arrester which is capable of doing this, is the electrolytic, or aluminum arrester In its usual form (cone or disc type) it comprises a series of cone-shaped aluminum cells, connected between line and ground through a spark gap. As soon as the voltage of the system rises above normal, by the value for which the spark gap is set, a discharge takes place through the aluminum cells, over a path of practically no resistance; but the volume of the discharge which passes, is not that given by the voltage on the system, but is merely that due to the excess voltage over the normal, since the normal voltage is held back by the counter e m.f of the aluminum cells As a result—with strokes following each other, thousands per second, that is, with a recurrent surge—the aluminum arrester discharges continuously; but it can stand the continuous discharge for half an hour or more without damage, since it does not carry the short-circuit current of the system, but merely the short-circuit current of the excess voltage, and so protects the circuit against continuous lightning for a sufficiently long time, until the cause of the high voltage can be found and eliminated.

The same characteristics as that of the aluminum arrester, is given by the Oxide Film Arrester. This differs from the aluminum arrester, in that it uses no liquid, and requires no charging.

Even the cone type of aluminum arrester discharges with a slight shock on the system, as the voltage must rise to

the value of the spark gap, before the discharge begins, and
an arrester having no spark gap, would therefore be very
desirable, especially in systems, in which even a small
voltage shock is objectionable, as mainly in large underground cable systems.

Of other forms of lightning arresters, the magnetic blowout 500-volt railway arrester is still in use to a large extent,
but is beginning to be superseded by the aluminum cell.
The multi-gap, being based on the non-arcing or rectifying
property of the metal cylinders which exists only with
alternating current, is not suitable for direct-current
circuits. In arc-light circuits, that is, constant-current
circuits, horn gap arresters with series resistance are
generally used, especially on direct-current arc circuits,
in which the multi-gap is not permissible. In such circuits of limited current, and very high inductance, the
series resistance is not objectionable Otherwise the horn
gap arrester is still occasionally used outdoors as emergency
arrester on transmission lines, set for a much higher
discharge voltage than the station arrester, and then
preferably without series resistance, but in such use, is a
serious menace to the system, due to the possibility of the
arc discharge setting off destructive oscillations.

Horn gaps with series resistance are to some extent
used on transmission lines as a cheap form of arresters,
in smaller substations, branch lines, etc., where the cost
of apparatus is not sufficient to justify the aluminum arrester. Such arrester naturally gives partial protection
only, against lightning disturbances of moderate power.

Protection of electric circuits is required against excess
currents, against excess voltages, and against excess
frequencies, including impulses of steep wave front

The protection against excess currents is afforded by

fuses, circuit-breakers and in general by limiting the power which may be concentrated at any point of the system, and in the huge modern electric power-generating systems, the judicious use of reactance in generators, busbars and feeders has solved the problem of limiting the possible power concentration to values within the control of automatic circuit-breakers, without interfering with the parallel operation of the entire system and without limiting the size of the system

Overvoltage protection is afforded by the lightning arresters, as discussed above.

Against high frequency and steep wave fronts, such lightning arresters can obviously protect only, if the high frequency is of such high voltage as to discharge over the lightning arrester; but where this is not the case, that is, where the high-frequency voltage is not sufficient to discharge over the spark gap of the lightning arrester, the latter obviously cannot protect

With the increasing size of the electric systems, and their increasing electrostatic capacity, in cables, high-potential overhead lines, etc , high-frequency phenomena or impulses of steep wave front are, however, becoming increasingly frequent, are indeed the most serious disturbances affecting such electric systems.

While the voltage of the high-frequency disturbance may not be sufficiently high to damage the insulation between the electric circuit and the ground, the serious danger of high frequency is the backing up of voltage across inductive parts of the circuit, such as transformer and generator windings, especially the end turns near the terminals, which receive the high frequency; series coils of voltage regulators; current transformers, etc.   The destruction caused by high frequency then is a local breakdown between turns or coils, resulting in a short-circuit thereof and frequently leading to the destruction of the apparatus by the heat of the excessive local short-circuit current.

Inductance exerts a barrier action against high frequency, and, when located at the entrance from the line into the station, more or less keeps high frequency out of the station, by reflecting it back into the line It thus exerts a protecting action against high frequency from the line, but at the same time becomes a serious danger in case of high frequency originating in the station, as by switching: it then reflects the high frequency back into the station instead of allowing it to pass into the line where it is dissipated in the line resistance. However, such barrier inductances usually are economically feasible only for very high frequency such as produced by lightning, of many hundred thousands of cycles. At lower frequencies, for instance, at the frequencies met in the stationary waves or cumulative oscillations of high-potential high-power transformers—of 20,000 to 100,000 cycles—the required amount of inductance becomes so large as to be economically impracticable.

Capacity shunting the circuit is effective in shunting high frequency, and absorbs the initial steep wave front of an impulse, which by its high-voltage gradient in inductance is so destructive, and thereby flattens out the wave front.

Resistance absorbs the high frequency or impulse energy.

The most effective protection against high-frequency oscillations and against sudden impulses of steep wave front, therefore, is afforded by a combination of capacity and resistance: the resistance, in shunt to the circuit, absorbs the high-frequency energy, and a capacity in series to the resistance keeps the low-frequency machine current from flowing through the resistance shunt, while it allows the high-frequency to pass unobstructed. Thus such combination of resistance and capacity acts as effective high-frequency absorber, and as such is extensively used, alone or in combination with the barrier action of an inductance ' In flattening the wave front and thereby protecting apparatus from "spilling over" by the sudden voltages of a very steep wave front, capacity without any resistance in series thereto is most effective, while for high-frequency energy dissipation, resistance is required in addition to the capacity.

TWELFTH LECTURE

ELECTRIC RAILWAY

TRAIN CHARACTERISTICS

The performance of a railway consists of acceleration, motion and retardation, that is, starting, running and stopping.

The characteristics which the railway motor must possess, are:

1. Reliability

2. Limited available space, which permits less margin in the design, so that the railway motor runs at a higher temperature, and has a shorter life, than other electrical apparatus The rating of a railway motor is, therefore, entirely determined by its heating. That is, the rating of a railway motor is that output which it can carry without its temperature exceeding the danger limit. The highest possible efficiency is, therefore, aimed at, not so much for the purpose of saving a few per cent of power, but because the power lost produces heat and so reduces the motor output.

3 Very variable demands in speed   That is, the motor must give a wide range of torque and speed at high efficiency. This excludes from ordinary railway work the shunt motor and the induction motor, unless a radical change in the method of railroad operation is accepted.

The power consumed in acceleration usually is many times greater than when running at constant speed, and where acceleration is very frequent, as in rapid transit service, the efficiency of acceleration is, therefore, of foremost importance, while in cases of infrequent stops, as in long-distance and interurban lines, the time of acceleration is so small a part of the total running time, that the power consumed during acceleration is a small part of the total power consumption, and high efficiency of acceleration is, therefore, of less importance

Typical classes of railway service are:

1. Rapid transit, as elevated and subway roads in large cities

Characteristics are high speeds and frequent stops.

2. City surface lines, that is, the ordinary trolley car in the streets of a city or town.

Moderate speeds, frequent stops, and running at variable speeds, and frequently even at very low speeds, are characteristic.

3. Suburban and interurban lines. That is, lines leading from cities into suburbs and to adjacent cities, through less densely populated districts.

Characteristics are less frequent stops, varying speeds, and the ability to run at fairly high speeds as well as low speeds.

4 Long-distance and trunk line railroading.

Characteristics are: infrequent stops, high speeds, and a speed varying with the load, that is, with the profile of the road.

5. Special classes of service, as mountain roads and elevators

Characteristics are fairly constant and usually moderate speed, a constant heavy load, so that the power of acceleration is not so much in excess of that of free running, and usually frequent stops. This is the class of work which can well be accomplished by a constant-speed motor, as the three-phase induction motor, and where regeneration, that is, returning power as generator, on the down grade, is desirable

The rate of acceleration and rate of retardation is limited only by the comfort of the passengers, which in this country permits as high values as 2 to $2\frac{1}{2}$ miles per hour per second, that is, during every second of acceleration, the speed increases at the rate of 2 to $2\frac{1}{2}$ miles per hour, so that 1 second after starting a speed of 2 to $2\frac{1}{2}$ miles per hour, 5 seconds after starting a speed of 5×2 to $2\frac{1}{2} = 10$ to $12\frac{1}{2}$ miles per hour, etc, is reached

In freight service by electric locomotive, the permissible acceleration may be limited by the traction, that is, the slipping of the drive wheels of the locomotive, as the locomotive is a small part of the train weight only.

Steam trains give accelerations of $\frac{1}{2}$ mile per hour per second and less with heavy trains, due to the lesser maximum power of the steam locomotive

Speed-time Curves.—In rapid transit, and all service where stops are so frequent that the power consumed during acceleration is a large part of the total power, the speed-time curves are of foremost importance, that is, curves of the car-run, plotted with the time as abscissæ, and the speed as ordinate

Choose for instance, a maximum acceleration and maximum braking of 2 miles per hour per second, and assuming a retardation of $\frac{1}{4}$ mile per hour per second by friction (that is, assuming that the car slows down $\frac{1}{4}$ mile per second, when running light on a level track), if then the time of one complete run between two stations is given equal to AB in Fig 29, the simplest type of run consists of constant acceleration, from A to C, on the line Aa, drawn under a slope of 2 miles per hour per second, at C the power is shut off and the car coasts on the slope CD, of $\frac{1}{4}$

mile per hour per second, until at D, where the coasting
line cuts the braking line bB (which also is drawn at the
slope of 2 miles per hour per second), the brakes are applied
and the car comes to rest, at B.   As the distance traveled is
speed times time, the area $ACDB$ so represents the distance
traveled, that is, the distance between the two stations,
and all speed-time curves of the same type, therefore, must
give the same area.   During acceleration, energy is put
into the car, and stored by its momentum, which is pro-

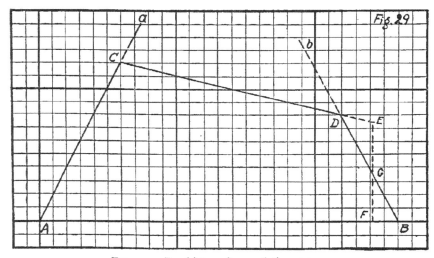

FIG. 29.—Rapid transit speed-time curve.

portional to the weight of the car and the square of the
speed.   It is, therefore, at a maximum at C.   A part of
the energy represented by the car speed is consumed during coasting in overcoming the friction; the rest is destroyed by the brakes.   Assuming, as approximation, constant friction, the energy consumed by the car friction on
the track, for runs of the same distance, is constant, and
the energy destroyed by the brakes is represented by the
speed at the point B, where the brakes are applied.   The
lower, therefore, this point B is, the less power is destroyed

by the brakes, and the more efficient is the run. More accurately, by prolonging *CD* to *E* so that area *DEG* = *BFG*, the area *ACEF* also is the distance between the stations, and *EF* so would·be the speed at which the car arrives at the next station, if no brakes were applied, and the energy corresponding thereto has to be destroyed by the brakes; that is, represents the energy lost during the run, and should be made as small as possible, to secure efficiency

The ratio of the energy used for carrying the car across the distance between the stations—that is, energy consumed by track friction, (plus energy consumed in climbing grades, where such exist) to the total energy input, that is, track friction plus energy consumed in the brakes, is the *operation efficiency* of the run

As an illustration, a number of such runs, for constant time of the run, of 130 seconds, and constant distance between the stations, that is, constant area of the speed-time diagram, are plotted in Figs 29 to 37.

1. Constant acceleration of 2 miles per hour per second, coasting at ¼ mile per hour per second, and braking at 2 miles per hour per second. Here the energy consumed by the brakes is given by the speed *EF* = 34 5 miles per hour, while the maximum speed reached is 60 miles per hour

2. Acceleration and retardation at 2 miles per hour per second. Constant speed running between Fig 30 Compared with 1 (which is shown in 30 in dotted lines), the maximum speed is slightly reduced, *e g.*, to 51 miles per hour, but the speed of application of the brakes, and therefore the energy lost in the brakes, is increased. That is, running at constant speed, between acceleration and braking, is less efficient than coasting with decreasing speed. Besides this, at the low power required for constant speed running, the motor efficiency usually is already lower.

It, therefore, is uneconomical to keep the power on the motors after acceleration, and more economical to continue to accelerate until a sufficient speed is reached to coast until the brakes have to be applied for the next station. Obviously, this is not possible where the distance between the stations is so great, that in coasting the speed would decrease too much to make the time, and so applies only to the case of runs with frequent stops, as rapid transit.

3. Constant acceleration of 1 mile per hour per second, braking at 2 miles, coasting ¼ mile. Diagram 1 is shown

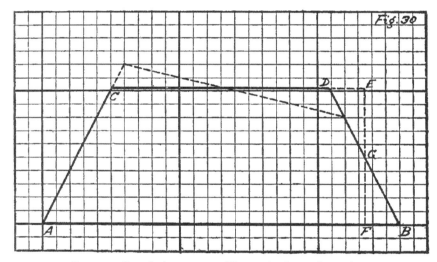

FIG. 30.—Speed-time curve with constant speed running.

in the same Fig. 31, for comparison. As seen, with the lower rate of acceleration, the maximum speed is greater, and the lost speed, or speed *EF*, which is destroyed by the brakes, is greater, that is, the efficiency of the run is lower.

4. Constant acceleration and braking of 1 mile per hour per second, coasting at ¼ mile. In this case, the run between the stations cannot be made in 130 seconds. For comparison, 1 is shown dotted in Fig. 32. Here the maximum speed and the lost speed are still greater, that is,

the efficiency of the run still lower, and at least 145 seconds are required. That is, the higher the rate of acceleration

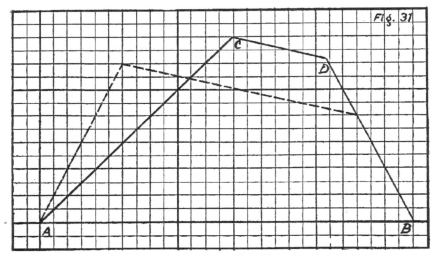

FIG. 31.—Slow acceleration speed-time curve.

and of braking, the less is the maximum speed required, and the higher the operation efficiency. With constant

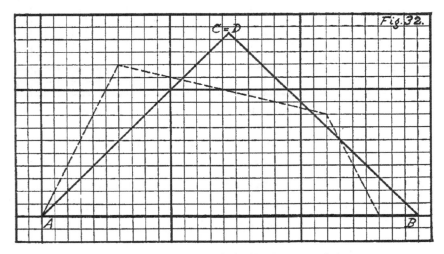

FIG. 32.—Slow acceleration and slow braking speed-time curve.

acceleration up to the maximum speed, the operation, therefore, is the more efficient the higher a rate of acceleration and of braking is used.   While very rapid acceleration requires more power developed by the motor and put into the car, the time during which the power is developed is so much shorter, that the energy put into the car, or power times time of power application, is less than with the lower rate of acceleration

The highest operation efficiency, in the case of frequent stops, therefore, is produced by constant acceleration at the highest permissible rate, coasting without power, and then braking at the highest permissible rate, as given by 1

During acceleration at constant rate, A to C, the motor, however, runs on the rheostat   That is, at all speeds below the maximum, to produce the same pull as at the maximum speed C, the motor consumes the same current and so the same power; while the power which it puts into the train is proportional to the speed, and therefore is very low at low speeds.   Or, in other words, the motor during constant acceleration, consumes power corresponding to maximum speed, while the useful power corresponds to the average speed, which during AC is only half the maximum, and so only half the available power is put into the car, the other half being wasted in the resistance, and the *motor efficiency* during constant acceleration, therefore, must be less than 50 per cent.

Constant acceleration up to maximum speed, while giving the best operation efficiency, so gives a very poor motor efficiency and thereby low total efficiency (the total efficiency being the ratio of the useful energy to the total energy put into the motors, that is, it is operation efficiency times motor efficiency).

This is the arrangement necessary for a constant-speed motor, as the induction motor, but it does not give the best total efficiency, but a better total efficiency is produced by accelerating partly on the motor curve, that is, at a decreasing rate. This sacrifices some operation efficiency, but increases the motor efficiency greatly and so, if not carried too far, increases the total efficiency.

The speed-time curves of the motor are shown in Fig. 33, and the current consumption is also plotted in this figure. Acceleration is constant from A to M, on the rheostat, and

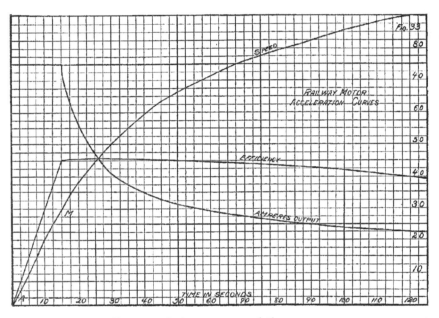

Fig. 33.—Series motor speed-time curve.

at constant-current consumption, from M, onward, the acceleration decreases, first slightly, then faster, but the current also decreases, first rapidly, and then more slowly; and the efficiency, plotted in Fig. 33, rises from o per cent. at A, to 90 per cent. at M, and then remains approximately constant, while the speed still increases.

6. This gives the speed-time curve of the car, Fig. 34, with acceleration on the motor curve and with maximum values of acceleration and braking 2, the coasting value

one-quarter; that is, the same as 1, and 1 is shown in dotted lines in the same figure. The acceleration is constant, on the rheostat, from A to M; at M the rheostat is cut out, and the acceleration continues on the motor curve, at a gradually decreasing rate, until at C the power is shut off and the car coasts until the brakes are applied. The area $AMCDB$, representing the distance between the stations, is the same as in 1; the operation efficiency is somewhat

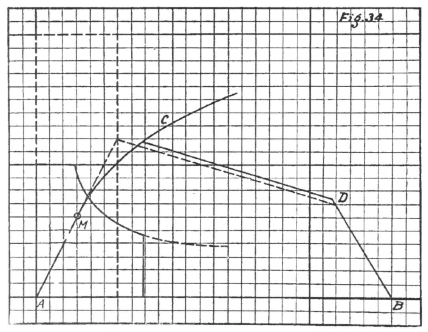

FIG. 34.---Series motor speed-time curve.

lower, but the total current consumption, as shown by the curves of current, shown together with the speed-time curves, is much less, and the power consumption, therefore, is less; that is, the total efficiency is higher.

7. Fig. 35 gives another speed-time curve in which, however, the motor is geared for too low a speed; so the motor curve is reached too early, and the power has to be kept on for too long a time, to make the run in time. As seen from

the current curves, here the loss in car efficiency by the decreased acceleration on the motor curve is greater than the saving in motor efficiency, and the power consumption by the motor is greater than that without running on the motor curve.

That is, the total efficiency of operation is increased by doing some of the accelerating on the motor curve, but may be impaired again by carrying this too far. Usually the rheostat is all cut out and the acceleration continues on the motor curve, from about half speed onward.

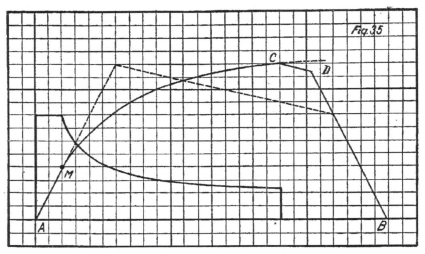

FIG. 35.—Inefficient speed-time curve.

8. During the first half of the acceleration on the rheostat, when more than half the voltage is consumed in the rheostat, half the current can be saved by connecting two motors in series; that is, by series parallel control on the motors, as shown in Fig. 36. If, however, the series connection of motors is maintained too long, as shown in Fig. 37, so that the part of the curve *SP* gets too long, the average rate of acceleration, and so the operation efficiency, is greatly reduced. That is, the lost area becomes so large, that the speed at application of the brakes, and so

the power lost in brakes, is greatly increased. Series
connection of motors, for efficient acceleration, therefore

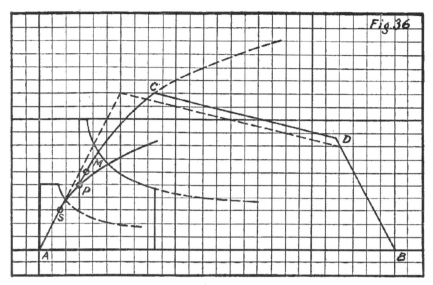

FIG. 36.—Efficient series-parallel control.

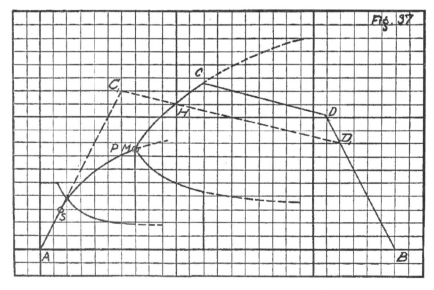

FIG. 37.—Inefficient series-parallel control.

should not be maintained for any length of time after the
rheostat has been cut out.

In series parallel control, as shown in Figs. 36 and 37, some acceleration occurs on the motor curve in series connection   That is, AS is acceleration on the rheostat, in series connection, SP acceleration on the motor curve, PM on the rheostat in parallel connection, and MC on the motor curve in parallel connection   Compared with 1, which is shown dotted in 37, the area $ASPMHC_1$ is lost; and so the equal area $HCDD_1$, has to be gained, giving a higher speed of application of the brakes D, but gaining power more than the increased power consumption in the brakes, by the higher motor efficiency.

CONCLUSION

In short-distance runs the efficiency is highest in running on series parallel control as much as possible on the motor curve, with as high a rate of average acceleration and retardation as possible, and coasting between acceleration and retardation; that is, not keeping the power on longer than necessary.

The longer the distance, the less important is high rate of acceleration and retardation, and for long-distance running the rate of acceleration and retardation is of little importance

Therefore, speed-time curves are specially important in rapid transit service, and in general, in running with frequent stops.

The heating of the motor at high acceleration, that is, with large current, is less than with low acceleration, that is, smaller current, because the current is on a much shorter time.

Feeding back in the line by using the motors as generators is rarely used in rapid transit, because with an efficient speed-time curve, using coasting, the speed when putting on the brakes is already so low that usually not enough power can be saved to compensate for the complication and the increased heating of the motors, when carrying current also in stopping. The motors are occasionally used as brakes, operating as generators on the rheostat. This, however, puts an additional heating on the motors; and is therefore not much used in this country, where the highest speed which the motor equipment can give is desired.

In long-distance railroading, however, and especially in mountainous regions, feeding back offers many advantages, not only in saving power, but in saving brakes, and in better train control and higher safety, and methods of feeding power back on down grades, of "regeneration," are increasingly becoming of importance in long-distance railroading.

With induction motors, feeding back in the line is simplest, because induction motors become generators above synchronism, and so feed back when running down a long hill. Therefore on mountain railways, induction motors have the advantage.

In an induction motor there is no running on the motor curve, and so the efficiency of acceleration is lower.

Objection to the series motor is the unlimited speed; that is, when running light, it runs away. In railroading this is no objection, because the motor is never running light and somebody is always in control.

In elevator work the series motor is objectionable, due to the unlimited speed, therefore, a limited-speed motor is necessary. In elevators frequent stops, and so efficient acceleration are necessary, therefore, a compound motor is best, that is, a motor having a shunt field to limit the speed and a series field (which is cut out after starting) to give efficient acceleration.

THIRTEENTH LECTURE

ELECTRIC RAILWAY: MOTOR CHARACTERISTICS

The economy of operation of a railway system, station, lines, etc , decreases and the amount of apparatus, line copper, etc., which is required, increases with increasing fluctuations of load, the best economy of an electric system therefore requires as small a power fluctuation as possible.

The pull required of the railway motor during acceleration, on heavy grades, etc , is, however, many times greater than in free running. In a constant-speed motor, as a direct-current shunt motor or an alternating-current induction motor, the power consumption is approximately proportional to the torque of the motor and thus to the drawbar pull that is given by it. With such motors, the fluctuation of power consumption would thus be as great as the fluctuation of pull required. In a varying-speed motor, as the series motor, the pull increases with decreasing speed, and the power consumption, which is approximately proportional to pull times speed, varies less than the pull of the motor The fluctuation of load produced in the circuit by a series motor therefore is far less than that produced by a shunt or induction motor—the former economizing power at high pull by a decrease of speed; the series motor thus gives a more economical utilization of apparatus and lines than the shunt or induction motor, and is therefore almost exclusively used.

The torque, and so the pull produced by a motor, is approximately proportional to the field magnetism and the

143

armature current; that is, neglecting the losses in the motor, or assuming 100 per cent. efficiency, the torque is proportional to the product of magnetic field strength and armature current.

In a shunt motor, at constant supply voltage e, the field exciting current, and thus the field strength, is constant; and the torque, when neglecting losses, is thus proportional to the armature current, as shown by the curve T_o in Fig. 38. From this torque is subtracted the torque consumed

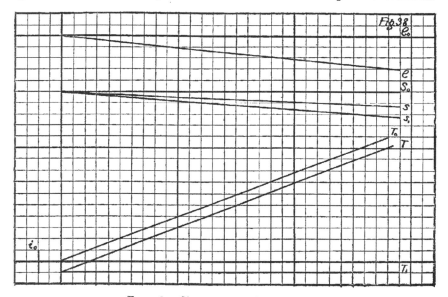

FIG. 38.—Shunt motor characteristic.

by friction losses, core loss, etc. (which, at approximately constant speed and field strength, is approximately constant and is shown by the curve T_1) thus giving as net torque of the motor, the curve T. Neglecting losses, the speed of the motor would be constant, as given by line S_o, since at constant field strength, to consume the same supply voltage e_o, the armature has to revolve at the same speed. As, however, with increasing load and therefore increasing current, the voltage available for the rotation of the armature decreases by the *ir* drop in the armature, as shown by the curve *e*; at constant field strength the speed decreases in the same proportion, as shown by the curve S_1. The field strength, however, does not remain perfectly constant, but with increasing load the field magnetism slightly changes: it decreases by field distortion and demagnetization, and the speed therefore increases in the same proportion, to the curve *S*. The current used as abscissæ in Fig. 38 is the armature current. The total current consumed by the

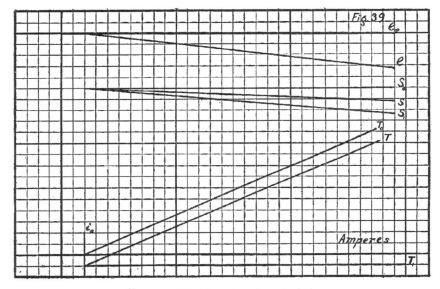

FIG. 39.—Shunt motor characteristic.

motor is, however, slightly greater, namely, by the exciting current i_o; and, plotted for the total current of the motor as abscissæ, all the curves in Fig. 38 are therefore shifted to the right, by the amount of i_o, as shown in Fig. 39.

If in the shunt motor, the supply voltage changes, the field strength, which depends upon the supply voltage, also changes; it decreases with a decrease of the supply voltage, and the current required to produce the same torque therefore increases in the same proportion. If the magnetic

10

field is below saturation, the field strength decreases in proportion to the decrease of supply voltage, and the current thus increases in proportion to the decrease of supply voltage, while the speed remains the same, the armature produces the lower voltage by revolving in the lower field at the same speed   If the magnetic field is highly oversaturated and does not therefore appreciably change with a moderate change of supply voltage and so of field current, the armature current required to produce the same torque also does not appreciably change with a moderate drop of supply voltage, but the speed decreases, since the armature must now consume less voltage in the same field strength.

Depending on the magnetic saturation of the field: with a decrease of the supply voltage the current consumed by the shunt motor to produce the same torque, therefore increases the more, the lower the saturation, and the speed decreases the more, the higher the saturation.

In general, a drop of voltage in the resistance of lines and feeders does not much affect the speed of the shunt motor, but increases the current consumption, thus still further increasing the drop of voltage; so that in a shunt-motor system, lines and feeders must be designed for a lower drop in voltage than is permissible for a series motor.

The induction motor in its characteristics corresponds to a shunt motor with undersaturated field, except that the effect of a drop of voltage is still more severe; as not only the amount, but usually the lag of current also increases, thus causing more drop in voltage; and the maximum torque of the motor is limited, and decreases with the square of the voltage   Hence, while in a series-motor system the lines and feeders are designed for the average load or average voltage drop (and practically no limit exists to the permissible maximum voltage drop), with an induction motor, the maximum permissible voltage drop is limited by the danger of stalling the motors.

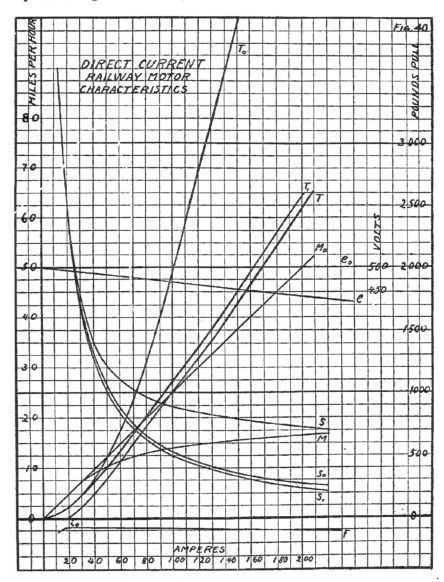

FIG. 40.—Series motor characteristic

In the series motor, the armature current passes through the field, and with increasing load and thus increasing current, the field strength also increases, the torque of the motor therefore increases in a greater proportion than the current. Neglecting losses and saturation, the field strength is proportional to the current, the torque being proportional to the current times field strength, therefore is proportional to the square of the current, as shown by the curve T_o in Fig 40. The supply voltage, however, has no direct effect on the torque, but with the same current consumption, the motor gives the same torque, regardless of the supply voltage. The speed, at constant supply voltage, changes with the field strength and thus with the current the higher the field strength, the lower is the speed at which the armature consumes the voltage Since the field strength—neglecting losses and saturation—is proportional to the current, the speed of the series motor would be inversely proportional to the current, as shown by the curve S_o in Fig 40.

As the voltage available for the armature rotation decreases with increasing current, from e_o to e, by the ir drop in the field and armature, the speed decreases in the same proportion, from the curve S_o to the curve S_1

In reality, however, the field strength, as shown by the curve M_o, is proportional to the current only at low currents; but for higher currents the field strength drops below, by magnetic saturation, as shown by the curve M; and ultimately, at very high currents, it becomes nearly constant. In the same ratio as the field strength drops below proportionality with the current, the speed increases and the torque decreases. The actual speed curve is therefore derived from the curve S_1 by increasing the values of the curve S_1 in the proportion, M_o to M, and is given by the curve S, and in the same proportion the torque is decreased to the curve T_1. From this torque curve the lost torque is now subtracted; that is, the torque representing the power consumed in friction and gear losses, hysteresis and eddy currents, etc   Some of the losses of power are approximately constant, others are approximately proportional to the square of the current, and the lost torque, being equal to the power loss divided by the speed, can therefore be assumed as approximately constant: somewhat higher at low and high speeds, as shown by curve F. The net torque then is given by the curve T. As seen, it is approximately a straight line, passing through a point i_o, which is the "running light current," and its corresponding speed, the "free running speed" of the motor.   At this current i_o, the speed is highest, with increase of current it drops first very rapidly, and then more slowly; and the higher the saturation of the motor field is, the slower becomes the drop of speed at high currents.

The single-phase alternating-current motors are either directly or inductively series motors, and so give the same general characteristics as the direct-current series motor. In the alternating-current motors, however, in addition to the ir drop an ix drop exists; that is, in addition to the voltage consumed by the resistance, still further voltage is consumed by self-induction; and the voltage e available for the armature rotation thus drops still further, as seen in Fig. 41. Since the self-induction consumes voltage in quadrature with the current, the inductive drop is not proportional to the current, but is small at low currents, and greater at high currents; e therefore is not a straight line, but curves downward at higher currents   The speed, S_1, is dropped still further by the inductive drop of voltage, to the curve S_1, and then raised to the curve S by saturation   The effect of saturation in the alternating-current motor usually is far less, since the magnetic field is alternating, and good power factor requires a low field excitation, and therefore high saturation cannot well be reached.

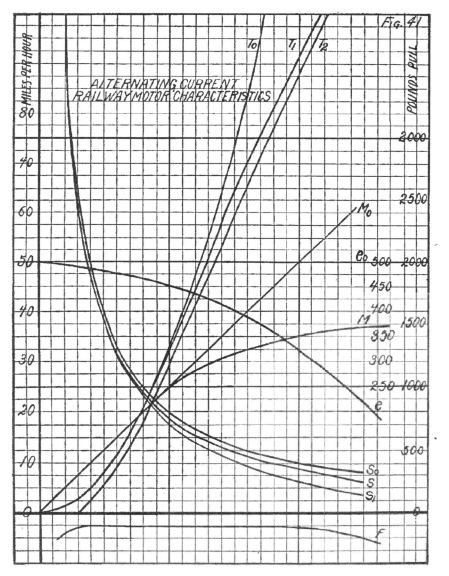

FIG. 41.—Alternating current series motor characteristic.

The torque curves are the same as in the direct-current motor, except that the effect of saturation is less marked.

In efficiency, the shunt or induction motor, and the series motor are about equal, and both give high values of efficiency over a wide range of current. A wide range of current, however, represents a wide range of speed in the series motor, and nearly constant speed in the shunt motor; therefore while the series motor can operate at high efficiency over a wide range of speed, the shunt motor shows high efficiency only at its proper speed

In regard to the effect of a change of supply voltage, as is caused, for instance, by a drop of voltage in feeders and mains, the series motor reacts on a change of voltage by a corresponding change of speed, but without change of current; while the shunt motor and induction motor react on a change of supply voltage by a change of current, with little or no change of speed   As the limitation of a system usually is the current, at excessive overloads on the system, resulting in heavy voltage drop, the series motors run slower, but continue to move; while the induction motor is liable to be stalled.

FOURTEENTH LECTURE

ALTERNATING-CURRENT RAILWAY MOTOR

In a direct-current motor, whether a shunt or a series motor, the motor still revolves in the same direction, if the impressed e m f be reversed, as field and armature both reverse. Since a reversal of voltage does not change the operation of the motor, such a direct-current motor therefore can operate also on alternating current. With an alternating voltage supply, the field magnetism of the motor also alternates, the motor field must therefore be laminated, to avoid excessive energy losses and heating by eddy currents (currents produced in the field iron by the alternation of the magnetism) just as in the direct-current motor the armature must be laminated

In the alternating-current motor in addition to the voltage consumed by the resistance of the motor circuit and that consumed by the armature rotation, voltage is also consumed by self-induction, that is, by the alternation of the magnetism. The voltage consumed by the resistance represents loss of power, and heating, and is made as small as possible in any motor. The voltage consumed by the rotation of the armature, or "e m.f of rotation," is that doing the useful work of the motor, and so is an energy voltage, or voltage in phase with the current, just as the voltage consumed by the resistance is in phase with the current. The voltage consumed by self-induction, due to the alternation of the magnetism, or "e m f of alternation," is in quadrature with the current, or wattless, that is, it consumes no power, but causes the current to lag,

152

and so lowers the power factor of the motor; that is, causes the motor to take more volt-amperes than corresponds to its output, and so is objectionable

The useful voltage, or e m.f of rotation of the motor, is proportional to the speed, or rather the "frequency of rotation," f_o, it is proportional to the field strength F, and to the number of armature turns m. The wattless voltage, or self-induction of the field, is proportional to the frequency f, to the field strength F, and the number of field turns n. The ratio of the useful voltage to the wattless voltage therefore is $mf_o \div nf$, and to make the useful voltage high and the wattless voltage low, therefore requires as high a frequency of rotation f_o and as low a frequency of supply f, as possible. Thus the commutator motors of more than 25 cycles give poor power factors, and for a given number of revolutions f_o, which is number of revolutions per second times number of pairs of poles, therefore is the higher, the more poles the motor has. Hence a greater number of poles are generally used in an alternating-current than in a direct-current motor.

Good direct-current motor design requires a strong field and weak armature, to get little field distortion and therefore good commutation, that is high n and low m But such proportions, even at low supply frequency f and high frequency of rotation f_o, would give a hopelessly bad power factor, and thus a commercially impractical motor. In the alternating-current commutator motor, it is therefore essential to use as strong an armature and as weak a field (that is, as large a number of armature turns m and as low a number of field turns n) as possible. Very soon, however, a limit is reached in this direction, even if the greater field distortion and the resultant bad commutation were not to be considered the armature also has a self-induction; that is, the alternating magnetism produced by the current in the armature turns consumes a wattless e m f. This magnetism is small in a direct-current motor, but with many armature turns and few field turns it becomes quite considerable, and so, while a further decrease of the field turns and increase of the armature turns reduces the self-induction of the field—which varies with the square of the field turns—it increases the self-induction of the armature—which varies with the square of the armature turns There is thus a best proportion between armature turns and field turns, which gives the lowest total self-induction This is about in the proportion, armature turns m to field turns $n = 2 \div 1$; and at this proportion the power factor of the motor, especially at low and moderate speeds, is still very poor

In alternating-current commutator motors it is therefore essential to apply means to neutralize the armature self-induction and armature reaction, so as to be able to increase the proportion of armature turns to field turns sufficiently to get good power factors This is done by surrounding the armature with a stationary "compensating winding" closely adjacent to the armature conductors, located in the field pole faces, and traversed by a current opposite in direction to the current in the armature, and of the same number of ampere-turns, so that the armature ampere-turns and the ampere-turns of the compensating winding neutralize each other, and the armature reaction, that is, the magnetic flux produced by the armature current, and the self-induction caused by it, disappear

This compensating winding for neutralizing the armature self-induction was introduced by R. Eickemeyer in the early days of the alternating-current commutator motor, and since then all alternating-current commutator motors have it; so that the electric circuits of all alternating-current commutator motors comprise an armature winding A, a field winding F, and a compensating winding C.

Since the compensating winding cannot be identically at the same place as the armature winding (the one being located in slots in the pole faces, the other in slots in the armature face) there still exists a small magnetic flux produced by the armature winding· the "leakage flux," analogous to the leakage flux of the induction motor; and the number of armature turns cannot be increased indefinitely, otherwise the armature self-induction, due to this leakage flux, would become appreciable, and the power factor would decrease again The minimum total self-induction of the motor with compensating winding occurs at a number of armature turns equal to three to five times the field turns; at this proportion, the power factor is already very good at low speeds, and the motor is industrially satisfactory in this regard.

For best results, that is, complete compensation and therefore zero magnetic field of armature reaction, it is, however, necessary not only to have the same number of ampere-turns in the compensating winding as on the armature, but also to have these ampere-turns distributed in the same manner around the circumference. With the usual armature winding this is not the case, but the armature conductors cover the whole circumference; while the compensating coil conductors cover only the pole arc, as the space between the poles is taken up by the field winding. That is, the magnetic distribution around the armature circumference is as shown developed in Fig. 42: the field gives a flat-topped distribution, the armature a peaked, and the compensating winding has a small flat top

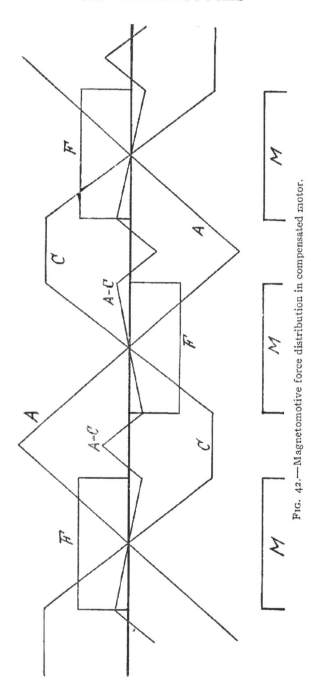

FIG. 42.—Magnetomotive force distribution in compensated motor.

and with the total ampere-turns of the compensating winding equal to those of the armature, the compensating winding preponderates in front of the field poles, the armature between the field poles, or at the brushes, and there is thus a small magnetic field of armature reaction remaining at the brushes, just where it is objectionable for commutation.

As it is not feasible to distribute the compensating winding over the whole circumference of the stator, the armature winding is arranged so that its ampere-turns cover only the pole arcs. This is done by using fractional pitch in the armature; that is, the spread of the armature coil or the space between its two conductors, is made, not equal to the pitch of the pole, as shown in Fig 43, but only to the pitch of the pole arcs, as shown in Fig 44 With such fractional pitch winding, the currents in the upper and the lower layer of the armature conductors, in the space between the poles, flow in opposite directions, and so neutralize, leaving only that part of the armature winding in front of the pole arcs as magnetizing. Hereby the distribution of the armature ampere-turns is made the same as that of the compensating winding, and so complete compensation is realized.

The compensating winding may be energized by the main current, and so connected in series with the field and armature, or the compensating winding may be short-circuited upon itself, and so energized by an induced current acting as a secondary of a transformer to the armature as primary; and as in a transformer, primary and secondary current have the same number of ampere-turns (practically) and flow in opposite directions, such "inductive compensation" is just as complete compensation as the "conductive compensation" produced by passing the main current through the compensating winding.

Vice versa, the armature may be short-circuited and so used as secondary of a transformer, with the compensat-

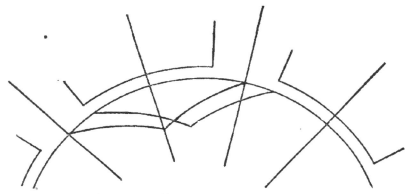

FIG. 43.—Full pitch armature winding.

ing winding acting as primary. In either of these motor types, which comprise primary and secondary circuits, that is, in which armature and compensating winding are

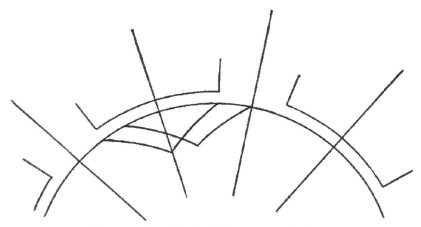

FIG. 44.—Fractional pitch armature winding.

not connected directly in series, but inductively, the field may be energized by the primary or supply current, or by the secondary or induced current. In such a motor embodying a transformer feature, instead of impressing the supply voltage upon one circuit as primary, while the other is closed upon itself as secondary, the supply voltage may be divided in any proportion between primary and secondary.

As primary and secondary current of a transformer are proportional to each other, it is immaterial, regarding the variation of the current in the different circuits with the load and speed, whether the circuits are directly in series, or by transformation; that is, all these motors have the same speed—torque—current characteristics, as discussed in the preceding lecture, and differ only in secondary effects, mainly regarding commutation.

The use of the transformer feature also permits, without change of supply voltage, to get the effect of a changed supply voltage, or a changed number of field turns, by shifting a circuit over from primary to secondary or *vice versa*. For instance, if the armature is wound with half as many turns, that is, for half the voltage and twice the current, as the compensating winding, by changing the field from series connection with the compensating winding to series connection with the armature, the current in the field and thus the field strength, is doubled; that is the same effect is produced as would be by doubling the number of field turns.

According to the relative connection of the three circuits, armature A, compensating circuit C, and field F, alternating-current commutator motors of the series type can be divided into the classes shown diagramatically in Fig 45

Primary.   Secondary

$A + C + F$ ———   Conductively Compensated Series Motor (2).

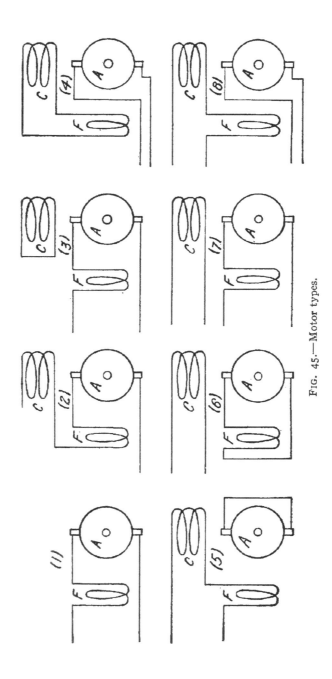

Fig. 45.—Motor types.

$A + F$	C	Inductively Compensating Series Motor (3).
A	$C + F$	Inductively Compensating Series Motor with Secondary Excitation, or Inverted Repulsion Motor (4)
$C + F$	A	Repulsion Motor (5).
C	$A + F$	Repulsion Motor with Secondary Excitation (6).
$C \& A + F$		Series Repulsion Motor A (7)
$C + F \& A$		Series Repulsion Motor B (8).

The main difference between these types of motors is found in their commutation.

In a direct-current motor, with the brushes set at the neutral, that is, midway between the field poles (as is customary in a reversible motor like the series motor), the armature turn, which is short-circuited under the brush during the commutation, encloses all the lines of magnetic force of the field, so during this moment it does not cut any lines of force by its rotation, and thus no e.m f is induced in this turn, that is, no current is produced, if the armature reaction is compensated for, or is otherwise negligible. If the motor has a considerable armature reaction, and thus a magnetic field at the brushes, this magnetic field of armature reaction induces an e.m.f. in the short-circuited turn under the brush, and so causes sparking. Hence high armature reaction impairs the commutation of the motor.

In an alternating-current series motor the armature

11

reaction is neutralized by the compensating winding, and therefore no magnetic field of armature reaction exists, hence no e.m f. is induced in the turn short-circuited under the brush by its rotation through the magnetic field.   As this field, however, is alternating, an e.m.f. is induced in the short-circuited turn by the alternations of the lines of magnetic force enclosed by it, and causes a short-circuit current and in that way, sparking   This e m f , being due to the alternation of the enclosed field flux, is independent of the speed of rotation, it also exists with the motor at a standstill, and is a maximum in the armature turn under the brush, as this encloses the total field flux. The position of the armature turn during commutation, which in a direct-current motor is the position of zero induced e.m.f , is therefore in an alternating-current motor, the position of maximum induced e.m.f., but induced not by the rotation of the turn, but by the alternation of the magnetism.   That is, this turn is in the position of a short-circuited secondary to the field coil of the motor as primary of a transformer, and as primary and secondary ampere-turns in a transformer are approximately equal, the current in the armature turn during commutation is very large, if not limited by the resistance or reactance of the coil, it is as many times greater than the full-load current, as the field coil has turns.   This causes serious sparking, if not taken care of

One way of mitigating the effect of this short-circuit current is to reduce it by interposing resistance or reactance; that is by making the leads between the armature turns and the commutator bars of high resistance or high reactance.   Obviously this arrangement can merely somewhat reduce the sparking by reducing the current in the short-circuited coil, but can not eliminate it; and it has the disadvantage, that in the moment of starting, if the motor does not start at once, the resistance lead is liable to be burned out by excessive heating, while when running, each lead is in circuit only a very small part of the time: during the moment when the armature turn to which it connects, is under a commutator brush. As the resistance of the lead must be very much greater than that of the armature coil, and as the space available for it is very much smaller, if remaining in circuit for any length of time it is destroyed by heat

In direct-current motors, commutation may be controlled by an interpole or commutating pole; that is, by producing a magnetic field at the brush, in direction opposite to the field of armature reaction, and by this field inducing in the armature turn during commutation, an e m f of rotation which reverses the current. Such commutating, poles are becoming extensively used in larger direct-current railway motors Such a commutating pole, connected in series into a circuit, would, in the alternating-current motor, in-induce an e m f in the short-circuited turn, by its rotation, but this e m.f. would be in phase with the field of the commutating pole, and thus with the current, that is, with the main field of the motor. Therefore it could not neutralize the e m f. induced in the short-circuited turn by the alternation of the main field through it, since this latter e.m f. is in quadrature with the main field, and thus with the current, but would simply add itself to it, and so make the sparking worse. A series commutating pole, while effective in a direct-current motor, is therefore ineffective in an alternating-current motor, due to its wrong phase

To neutralize the e.m f. induced by the alternation of the main field through the armature turn during commutation, by an opposite e.m.f. induced in this turn by its rotation through a quadrature field or commutating field, this field must therefore have the proper phase The e.m f of alternation of the main field through the short-circuited turn is proportional to the main field F and frequency f, and is in quadrature with the main field. The e.m f. induced in the short-circuited turn by its rotation through the commutating field is proportional to the frequency of rotation or speed f_o, and to the commutating field F_o, and in phase therewith; to be in opposition and equal to the e.m.f. of alternation, the commutating field must therefore be in quadrature with the main field, and frequency times main field must equal speed times commutating field That is

$$fF = f_oF_o$$

or in other words, the commutating field must be:

$$F_o = \frac{f}{f_o}F$$

or equal to the main field times the ratio of frequency to speed, and in quadrature therewith.

Hence, at synchronism: $f_o = f$, the commutating field must be equal to the main field; at half synchronism: $f_o = \frac{1}{2}f$, it must be twice, at double synchronism: $f_o = 2f$, it must be one-half the main field.

The problem of controlling the commutation of the alternating-current motor therefore requires the production of a commutating field of proper strength, in quadrature phase with the main field of the motor, and thus with the current.

In a transformer, on non-inductive or nearly non-inductive secondary load, the magnetism is approximately in quadrature behind the primary, and ahead of the secondary current, transformation between compensating winding and armature thus offers a means of producing a quadrature field in the alternating-current motor for compensation.

In the conductively compensated series motor, at perfect compensation, no quadrature field exists, while with over or undercompensation, a quadrature field exists, in phase with the current, and therefore not effective as commutating field.

In the inductively compensated series motor, the quadrature field, which transforms current from the armature to the compensating winding, is of negligible intensity, as the compensating winding is short-circuited, and thus consumes very little voltage

A quadrature field, however, appears in those motors in which the compensating winding is primary, and the armature secondary, that is in repulsion motors, since in the armature the induced or transformer e m f. is opposed by the e m.f of rotation, so a considerable e m f is induced, and therefore a considerable transformer flux exists.

Therefore, when impressing the supply voltage on the compensating winding, and short-circuiting the armature upon itself, that is, in the repulsion motor, the voltage is supplied to the armature by transformation from the compensating winding, and the magnetic flux of this transformer is in quadrature with the supply current; that is, it has the proper phase as commutating flux.

The repulsion motor thus has in addition to the main field, in phase with the current, a transformer field, in quadrature with the main field in space and in time, and so in the proper direction and phase as commutating field, thus giving perfect commutation if this transformer field has the intensity required for commutation, as discussed above.

As in the repulsion motor, the armature is short-circuited upon itself, the voltage supplied to it by transformation

from the compensating winding equals the voltage consumed in it by the rotation through the main field.   The
former voltage is proportional to the frequency f and to
the transformer field F^1, the latter to the speed f_o and to
the main field F, and it so is

$$fF^1 = f_oF,$$

that is, the transformer field is

$$F^1 = \frac{f_o}{f}F$$

or equal to the main field times the ratio of speed to
frequency.

Comparing this value of the transformer field of the repulsion motor, F^1, with the required commutating field F_o,
it is seen that at synchronism $f_o = f$, $F^1 = F_o$, that is, the
transformer field of the repulsion motor has the proper value
as commutating field, so that no short-circuit current is
produced in the armature turn under the brush, but the
commutation is as good as in a direct-current motor with
negligible armature reaction

At half synchronism, $f_o = \frac{1}{2}f$, the transformer field of
the repulsion motor $F^1 = \frac{1}{2}F$, is only one-quarter as large
as the commutating field required $F_o = 2F$, and the short-
circuit current is reduced by 25 per cent. below the value
which it has in the series motor, and the commutation, while
it is better, is not yet perfect.

At double synchronism: $f_o = 2f$, the transformer field
is $F^1 = 2F$, while the commutation field should be· $F_o =
\frac{1}{2}F$, and the transformer field thus is four times larger
than it should be for commutation; so that only one-quarter
of the transformer field is used to neutralize the e.m.f of
alternation in the short-circuited turn, the other three-
quarters induces an e m f , thus causing a short-circuit cur-

rent three times as large as it would be in a series motor. That is, the short-circuit current under the brush, and thus the sparking, in the repulsion motor at double synchronism is very much worse than in the series motor, and the repulsion motor at these high speeds is practically inoperative.

Hence, as regards commutation, a repulsion motor is equal to the series motor at standstill where no compensation of the short-circuit current is possible—but becomes better with increasing speed: as good as a good direct-current series motor at synchronism; and then again becomes worse by overcompensation, until at some speed above synchronism, it again becomes as poor as the alternating-current series motor; above this speed, it becomes rapidly inferior to the series motor.

To produce right intensity of the transformer field, to act as commutating field, it is therefore necessary above synchronism to reduce the transformer field below the value which it would have when transforming the total supply voltage from compensating winding to armature. This means, that above synchronism, only a part of the supply voltage must be transformed from compensating winding to armature, the rest directly impressed upon the armature. Thus at double synchronism, where the transformer field of the repulsion motor is four times as strong as is required for commutation, to reduce it to one-quarter, only one-quarter of the supply voltage must be impressed upon the compensating winding, three-quarters directly on the armature.

To get zero short-circuit current in the armature turn under the brush, below synchronism more than the full supply voltage would have to be impressed upon the compensating winding, which usually cannot conveniently be done. At synchronism the full supply voltage is im-

pressed upon the compensating winding, while the armature
is short-circuited as repulsion motor; and with increasing
speed above synchronism, more and more of the supply
voltage is shifted over from compensating winding to armature; that is, the voltage impressed upon the compensating
winding is reduced, from full voltage at synchronism, while
the voltage impressed upon the armature is increased, from
zero at synchronism, to about three-quarters of the supply ·
voltage at double synchronism.   Such a motor, in which the
transformer field is varied in accordance with the requirement of commutation, is called a "series repulsion motor"

The arrangement described here eliminates the short-circuit current induced in the commutated armature turn by
the alternation of the main field, and that completely above
synchronism, so that during commutation, no current is
induced in the armature turn   This, however, is not sufficient for perfect commutation: during the passage of the
armature turn under the brush, the current in the turn
should reverse; so that in the moment in which the turn
leaves the brush, the current has already reversed.   For
sparkless commutation, it therefore is necessary, in addition to the neutralizing e m f. of the transformer field, to
induce an e m f which reverses the current.   This e m f ,
and thus the magnetic flux which induces it by the rotation,
must be in phase with the current   That is, in addition
to the "neutralizing" component of the commutating
field (which is in quadrature with the current), to reverse
the current, a second component of the commutating field
must exist, in phase with the current; this component so
may be called the "reversing field."   The total commutating field required to eliminate the short-circuit current due
to the alternating main field by the "neutralizing" flux,
and to reverse the armature current by the "reversing

flux," must therefore be somewhat less than 90° lagging behind the main field and thus the main current

While in a transformer with non-inductive load on the secondary, the magnetic flux lags nearly 90° behind the primary current, in a transformer with inductive load on the secondary, the magnetic flux lags less than 90° behind the primary current, and the more so the higher the inductivity of the secondary load.

Therefore, by putting a reactance into the armature circuit of the motor, and so making the armature circuit inductive, the transformer flux is made to lag less than 90° behind the current, and act not only as neutralizing but also as reversing flux, and so, if it be of proper intensity, it gives perfect commutation

An additional reactance would in general be objectional, in lowering the power factor of the motor. The motor, however, contains a reactance· its field circuit, which has to be excited, can be used as reactance for the armature circuit. That is, by connecting the field coils into the armature circuit, or in other words, using secondary excitation, the transformer flux of the motor is given the lead ahead of quadrature position with the main field, which is required to act as reversing field. However, hereby the power factor of the motor is somewhat lowered.

In this manner, it is possible in the alternating-current commutator motor, to get at all speeds from synchronism upwards, the same perfect commutation as in a direct-current motor with commutating poles, by varying the distribution of supply voltage between compensating winding and armature, and exciting the field in series with the armature circuit; that is, in the series repulsion motor B of the preceding table Obviously, this distribution of voltage would for all practical purposes be carried out sufficiently

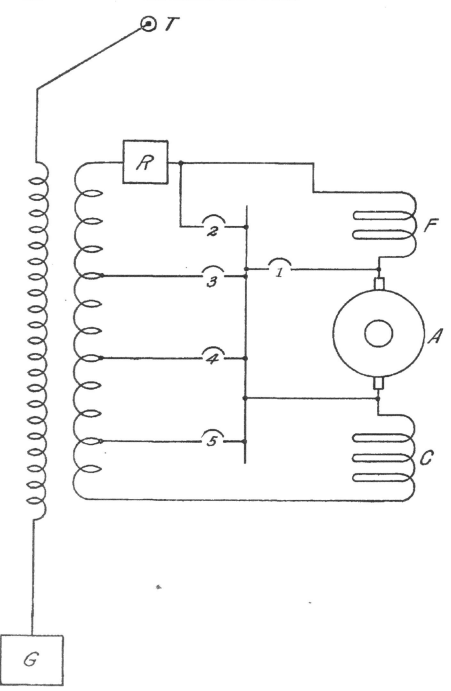

FIG. 46.

by using a number of steps, as shown diagrammatically by the arrangement in Fig. 46:

T is the supply circuit, F the field winding, A the armature, and C the compensating winding.

Closing switch 1, and leaving all others open, the motor is a repulsion motor.

Closing switch 2, and leaving 1 and all others open, the motor is a repulsion motor with secondary excitation

Closing switch 3, or 4, 5 . . and leaving all others open, the motor is a series repulsion motor B, with gradually increasing armature voltage and decreasing voltage on the compensating winding

By winding the armature for half the voltage and twice the current of the compensating winding, when changing from position 1, the field in the compensating circuit, to the next position, with the field in the armature circuit, the field current and the field' strength becomes double the value it had in starting, where no compensation exists, and which it would have to maintain in a series motor; and thus a correspondingly greater motor output is secured, than would be possible in a motor in which the commutation is not controlled.

FIFTEENTH LECTURE

ELECTROCHEMISTRY

Electrochemistry is one of the most important applications of electric power, and possibly even more power is used for electrochemical work than for railroading.

In electrochemical industries the most expensive part is electric power; material and labor are usually much less. Such industries therefore are located at water powers, where the cost of power is very low.

The main classes of electrochemical work are.

A. Electrolytic.

B. Electrometallurgical.

A. ELECTROLYTIC WORK

The chemical action of the current is used, by electrolyzing either solutions of salts or fused salts or compounds.

Electrolysis of solutions in water is possible only with such metals which have less chemical affinity than hydrogen. For instance, Cu, Fe, and Zn can be deposited from salt solutions in water, but not Al, Mg, Na, etc. Electrolyzing, for instance, NaCl (salt solution) the sodium (Na) which appears at the negative terminal immediately dissociates the water and gives $Na + H_2O = NaOH + H$, or: sodium plus water = caustic soda plus hydrogen.

It takes 1.4 volts to electrolyze water; any metal requiring more than 1 4 volts for separation therefore is not separated, but hydrogen is produced.

172

Therefore the highest voltage used in an electrolytic cell containing water is 1 4 + the *ir* drop in the resistance of the cell, which latter, for reasons of economy, is made as low as possible.

Even fused salts require fairly low voltage, at the highest from 3 to 4 volts.

Since the voltage required per cell is very low, a large number of cells are connected in series, and even then large low-voltage machines are required

Some of the important applications of electrolysis are

Electroplating, that is, covering with copper, nickel, silver, gold, etc.

Electrotyping, that is, making of copies, usually of copper, and especially

Metal refining.

A very large part of all the copper used is electrically refined. The crude copper as cast plate is used as anode or positive, and a thin plate of refined copper is used as cathode, or negative terminal in a copper sulphate solution The anode is dissolved by the current and the fine copper is deposited on the cathode; while silver and gold go down into the mud, lead goes into the mud as sulphate, tin as oxide; sulphur, selenium and tellurium, arsenic and other impurities also go in the mud, and zinc and iron remain in solution as sulphates if the current density is sufficiently low. If the current density is high, some zinc and iron may deposit · zinc and iron have a greater chemical activity than copper, since they precipitate copper from solution Therefore, it takes more power, that is, more voltage, to deposit zinc and iron, than it takes to deposit copper. If the current density is low, the voltage required to deposit the copper plus the *ir* drop, that is, the total voltage of the cell, is less than the voltage required to deposit zinc or iron, and they do not deposit, but dissolve at the anode and remain in solution.

At higher current density the *ir* drop in the cell is higher; thus the total voltage of the cell is higher, and may become high enough to deposit iron or even zinc

If the anode is crude copper, the cathode pure copper, the voltage at the anode is higher than at the cathode and the cell takes some voltage. The voltage required for copper refining is the higher, the more impure the copper is; but is always very low, usually a fraction of a volt, and therefore very many cells are run in series.

The solution gradually becomes impure and has to be replaced.

Other metals as zinc, lead, iron, etc., are occasionally refined electrolytically, but not to the same extent as copper.

Metal Reduction.—Metals are reduced from their ores electrolytically, especially such metals which have so high chemical affinity that they are not reduced by heating with carbon. In this way aluminum, magnesium, sodium, calcium, etc , are made electrolytically Since their chemical affinity is greater than that of hydrogen, they cannot be deposited from solutions in water, but only from fused salts, or solutions in fused salts So calcium is produced now by electrolyzing fused calcium chloride, $CaCl_2$. Aluminum is made by electrolyzing a solution of alumina in melted cryolite (sodium aluminum fluoride).

Secondary Products.—Frequently electrolysis is used to produce not the substances which are directly deposited, but substances produced by the reaction of these deposits on the solutions For instance, electrolyzing a solution of salt, NaCl, in water, we get sodium, Na, at the negative, chlorine, Cl, at the positive terminal.

If we use mercury, Hg, as negative electrode, it dissolves the sodium and so we get sodium amalgam.

Otherwise the sodium does not deposit but immediately acts upon the water and forms sodium hydrate or caustic soda, NaOH.

The chlorine, Cl, at the anode also reacts on the water, one chlorine atom taking up one hydrogen and another chlorine atom the remaining OH of the water, H_2O, that is, we get $2Cl + H_2O = ClH + ClOH$, that is, hydrochloric + hypochlorous acid

With the sodium hydrate from the other cathode these acids form NaCl and ClONa, that is sodium chloride and hypochlorite, or bleaching soda

If the solution is hot, the reaction goes further and we get $6Cl + 3H_2O = 5ClH + ClO_3H$, that is hydrochloric and chloric acid, and with the sodium hydrate from the other side these form NaCl and ClO_3Na, that is, sodium chloride and sodium chlorate

In this way considerable industries have developed, producing electrolytically caustic soda, bleaching soda, and chlorates

Alternating current is used very little for electrolytic work, as with organic compounds to produce oxidation and reduction at the same time, that is, act on the compound in rapid succession by oxygen and hydrogen, the one during the one, the other during the next half wave of current

Very active metals like manganese and silicon dissolve by alternating current, that is, one-half wave dissolves, but the other does not deposit again.

Very inert metals like platinum are deposited by alternating current, that is, the negative half wave deposits by alternating current, but the positive half wave does not dissolve.

B. ELECTROMETALLURGICAL WORK

In electrometallurgical work the heat is used to produce the chemical action, thus it is immaterial whether alternating or direct current is used

The voltage required is still low but not as low as in electrolytic work

The carborundum furnace takes from 250 to 90, mostly about 100 volts; that is, it starts cold with 250 volts. While heating up the resistance drops, and the voltage decreases down to 100 volts when the furnace is hot and remains there until toward the end. Then the inner layer of carborundum begins to change to graphite and the resistance, and therefore the voltage falls.

The carbide furnace and arc furnaces in general take from 50 to 100 volts, the graphite furnace takes from 10 to 20 volts.

To get very high temperatures a very large amount of energy has to be concentrated in one furnace; and with the moderate voltage used, this requires very large currents, thousands of amperes. Alternating currents are almost exclusively used, since it is easier to produce very large alternating currents by transformers, and since it is easier to control alternating than direct currents

Electric heat necessarily is very much more expensive than heat produced by burning coal, and so the electric furnace is used mainly

First —Where very perfect control of the temperatures and freedom from impurities is essential

Second —Where temperatures higher than can be produced by combustion are required.

1 Very accurate temperature regulation and freedom from impurities, for instance, are important in making and annealing high-grade tool steels, etc By using coal or oil

as fuel, contamination by the gases of combustion, and by the metal taking up carbon (or if an excess of air is used, oxygen) is difficult to avoid

By electric heating, by resistance at lower temperature and by induction furnace at higher temperature, contamination can be perfectly avoided and even the air can be excluded.

2. The temperature of combustion is limited.

Four-fifths of air is nitrogen which does not take part in the combustion, but which has to be heated, thus greatly lowering the temperature; therefore combustion in air, even if the air is preheated, gives a lower temperature than when using oxygen. But even the temperature of the oxy-hydrogen, or the oxy-acetylene flame is only just able to melt platinum

The temperature which can be reached by combustion, is limited, since at very high temperature the chemical affinity of oxygen for hydrogen and carbon ceases. water dissociates, that is, spontaneously splits up in hydrogen and oxygen at 2000°C. and no temperature higher than 2000° can therefore be reached by the oxy-hydrogen flame, carbon dioxide, CO_2, already dissociates at about 1500°C into carbon monoxide, CO, and oxygen, O. Carbon monoxide, CO, splits up into carbon and oxygen not much above 2000°C. (In all high temperature reactions of carbon, as in the formation of carbides, CO therefore always forms and not CO_2, since CO_2 cannot exist at a very high temperature, and the CO when leaving the furnace then burns to CO_2 with blue flame.)

Higher temperatures than those generated by the combustion of carbon and hydrogen can be produced by the combustion of those elements whose oxides are stable at very high temperatures, as aluminum and calcium In this way, many metals, as chromium and manganese, which

12

cannot be reduced from the oxides by carbon (due to the lower temperature of carbon combustion) can be reduced by aluminum in the "thermite" process. That is, their oxides are mixed with powdered aluminum and then ignited: the aluminum burns in taking up the oxygen of the metal, and so produces an extremely high temperature, which melts the metal and the alumina (corundum) which is produced.

Since, however, all the aluminum is made electrolytically, the thermite process still requires the use of electric power. The temperature of combustion of aluminum, however, is still far below that of the electric carbon arc, since in the carbon arc, alumina boils.

For temperatures above 2000° to 2500°C , and up to the arc temperature or about 3500°C , electric energy is therefore necessary

Electric furnaces are of two classes·

Arc Furnaces and Resistance Furnaces.

In the resistance furnace any temperature can be produced up to the point of destruction of the resistance material, that is, up to 3500°C., when using carbon.

The arc furnace gives the arc temperature of 3500°C., but allows the concentration of much more energy in a small space and thus produces reactions requiring the very highest · temperatures   .

Some of the electrometallurgical industries are:

(a) Calcium carbide production   Arc furnaces are used and the reaction is

$$CaO + 3C = CaC_2 + CO$$

A mixture of coke and quick lime is used in the process.

(b) Carborundum production   A resistance furnace is used, containing a carbon core about 24 feet long, around which the material is placed and heated by the current passing through the core   The furnace takes 1000 horse-power and the reaction is:

$$SiO_2 + 3C = SiC + 2CO$$

The material is a mixture of sand, coke, sawdust and salt.

(c) Graphite furnace. A resistance furnace somewhat similar to the carborundum furnace is used, but with lower voltage and larger currents; the material is coke or anthracite, which by the high temperature is converted into graphite, probably passing through an intermediate stage as a metal carbide.

(d) Silicon furnace   Either arc or resistance furnace is used, the reaction is

$$SiO_2 + 2C = Si + 2CO.$$

or,

$$SiO_2 + 2SiC = 3Si + 2CO.$$

(e) Titanium carbide furnace. Arc or resistance furnace is used which requires a very high temperature; that is, a greater temperature than that of the calcium carbide furnace.

$$TiO_2 + 3C = TiC + 2CO$$

Other products of the electric furnace are siloxicon, silicon monoxide, etc , and numerous alloys of refractory metals, mainly with iron, as of vanadium, tungsten, molybdenum, titanium, etc , which are used in steel manufacture.

In the steel industry, the electric furnace is finding a rapidly increasing use, in steel smelting

The use of the electric arc for the production of nitric acid and nitrate fertilizers, of the high-potential glow discharge for the production of ozone for water purification, etc , also are applications of electric power, which are of rapidly increasing industrial importance

SIXTEENTH LECTURE

THE INCANDESCENT LAMP

The two main types of electric illuminants are the incandescent lamp and the arc lamp.

In the incandescent lamp, the current flows through a solid conductor of practically constant resistance, usually in a vacuum, and the heat produced in the resistance of the conductor makes it incandescent, thus giving the light. Incandescent lamps in an electric circuit thus act as non-inductive ohmic resistances, and as such can be operated equally as well on constant-potential as on constant-current supply. As electric distribution systems are almost always constant-potential, most incandescent lamps are operated on constant-potential, usually in multiple on 110-volt secondary or lighting mains (one side of an Edison three-wire circuit). Only for street lighting, where the distances over which the lighting circuit extends, is too great to transmit constant potential at the low lamp voltage of 110, series connection of the incandescent lamps is used, and the lamps then are operated on constant-current direct or alternating-current circuits, in the same manner as arc lamps. However, even in series lighting by incandescent lamps, constant-potential systems are increasingly applied, that is, a large number—50 to 100 or more—incandescent lamps connected in series with each other, directly or through individual auto-transformers or transformers, into a constant-potential supply circuit, as this offers a higher efficiency and a much better power factor of the circuit. In this case, provisions have to be made, either by

180

protective devices or by suitable design of the auto-transformer, so that the burning out or failure of a lamp does not affect the other lamps of the series circuit. On constant current, not infrequently incandescent lamps are operated in series with arc lamps on the same circuits, though this is not good practice, as the incandescent lamp is far more sensitive to current and voltage fluctuations than the arc lamp, requiring a better regulation of the circuit, and circuit fluctuations, which would be harmless to arc lamps, may seriously impair the life of the incandescent lamps.

It is now nearly 40 years ago that the carbon-filament incandescent lamp was industrially developed by Edison, with its characteristic features carbon glowing in a vacuum perfectly glass enclosed and with platinum leading-in wires. Various previous attempts to use platinum and other materials as radiators had failed, due to their lower melting points. Very great differences were found in the efficiency of light production between the filaments produced by the carbonization of different vegetable fibers, and so an extensive search was started for the best fiber, and continued for years, and expeditions sent out all over the world to find the fiber which when carbonized was most stable, that is, could be operated at the highest temperature and corresponding efficiency of light production. This search ended somewhat tragically, for when finally a bamboo fiber had been found better than all previous ones, and brought back from the wilderness, a still better fiber had just been produced in the chemical laboratory, of squirted cellulose, and from then on, until in the last years the carbon filament became antiquated, squirted cellulose fibers have exclusively been used.

Pure cellulose—purified cotton—is dissolved, in zinc chloride or in cupric-ammon, or nitrocellulose in glacial acetic acid, and the thick molasses-like solution squirted through a fine hole, into some liquid, which takes up the solvent of the cellulose, and so hardens the fiber: alcohol with zinc chloride, diluted hydrochloric acid with cupric-ammon, water with acetic acid.   The horn-like and perfectly homogeneous and uniform fiber, which is thus produced, is then cut to size and carbonized   While fairly efficient, it is not as efficient as some forms of deposited carbon, and the carbonized cellulose filaments, "base filaments," as they are called, then are heated by an electric current in gasolene vapor under a partial vacuum Thereby a thin layer of a grayish carbon is deposited on the surface of the filament, which is more stable, thus permits operating such "treated filaments" at a higher efficiency than the original base filaments.

In the few years of Edison's work on the incandescent lamp, the carbon-filament lamp had been developed, from a conception ridiculed by most engineers, to such a perfection, that for nearly a quarter of a century no material and radical further improvements were made, but all the advance made in the carbon-filament incandescent lamp, from the days when it left Edison's hands, until nearly 25 years afterwards, essentially consisted in a steady slow improvement in manufacturing details, resulting in a great decrease of cost and increase of uniformity of the product, and as the result thereof a slow and gradual increase of efficiency, up to a specific consumption of 3.1 watts per candlepower   However, the improvement in the efficiency of the incandescent lamp, during the quarter of a century from the days of Edison's work up to the final replacement of the carbon lamp by the metal-filament lamp, was less than improvements in efficiency, which since have taken. place in a single year or two in metal-filament lamps.

Only one radical advance was made, fairly close to the last days of the carbon-filament lamp, by the development of a new form of carbon, by the electrochemical research laboratory of the G. E Co , the so-called "metallic carbon." This, produced from vapor deposited carbon at the highest temperature of the electric furnace, has many pronounced metallic characteristics. low resistivity, positive temperature coefficient, metallic luster, etc., and a much higher stability, which permitted increasing the efficiency of light production, in the so-called "Gem"[1] lamp, to 2 5 watts per candle. However, this efficiency was not sufficient to save the carbon filament in competition with the much more efficient metal filaments of today, and whether carbon as incandescent lamp filament has forever gone out of use, or whether some time some other form of carbon will be found, so much more stable that it can compete with the metal-filament lamps, remains in the future.

The first challenge of the supremacy of the carbon-filament incandescent lamp came from the Nernst lamp, claiming an efficiency twice as high as that of the carbon-filament lamp Developed by Professor Nernst in Germany, it was introduced and industrially adapted to our country's conditions. The light-giving glower of the Nernst lamp operates in air, requiring and permitting no vacuum It is a short rod of rare oxides, similar to those which constitute the Welsbach mantle, which has so greatly increased the efficiency of gas lighting. However, the Nernst lamp glower is not a dead resistance like a carbon filament or metal wire, but is a peculiar kind of conductor, a so-called "pyroelectric conductor," which has a number of electrical characteristics similar to those of the arc it cannot be

[1] An abbreviation of "G. E. Metallized "

operated on constant potential supply, but requires a steadying resistance or "ballast resistance," and it is not self-starting, but has to be started by heating, by means of a "heater spiral." As the result, the Nernst lamp is not as simple, but must contain auxiliary devices, ballast resistance and heater spiral, and mechanism to cut the heater spiral out of circuit after the glower has started. Herefrom, and from the high temperature of operation of the glower, formidable difficulties resulted in the commercial development of the lamp, and when finally engineering skill had carried the development so far as to commercially verify the claims of efficiency, especially in the larger units of the Nernst lamp, in the meantime the tungsten-filament lamp with its still much higher efficiency had made its appearance, and the Nernst lamp met the tragic fate of coming too late, and now has practically disappeared

The first real metal-filament lamp was the osmium lamp. It was developed abroad and introduced here to a limited extent only. It gave an efficiency of 1 3 to 1.6 watts per candle, with good life. Industrially, it was of no importance, as the total amount of osmium on earth would not be sufficient to supply one year's demand of incandescent lamps. Theoretically, however, it was of terrible significance, by sounding the death-knell of the carbon filament, in proving that metal filaments can be operated at more than twice the efficiency of the carbon filament, and while osmium was not available in sufficient quantities, it was not improbable that other suitable metals might be found, which are more plentiful. Osmium, while a metal, was never produced in a ductile state, and the osmium filament was made by a squirting process, similar to the carbon filament.

The search for refractory metals then led to the tantalum-filament lamp, and thus the tantalum incandescent lamp arose and began rapidly to displace the carbon filament—until in its turn it vanished before the tungsten-filament lamp of today

Tantalum is not as infusible as osmium, and therefore could not offer quite as high an efficiency as the osmium lamp. It gave, however, an efficiency of 2 watts per candle, hence a material advance even over the metallized carbon or Gem lamp. Tantalum is a rare metal, that is, it nowhere exists in large quantities, but it is not limited like osmium, but is found very plentifully in small quantities. It is a ductile metal, can be drawn into fine wire, and the tantalum lamp thus was the first wire-wound lamp: that is, the metal is drawn into a fine wire of the required diameter, the required length cut off, and then wound on a framework in the lamp bulb. As the result of using drawn wire, peculiar difficulties, resulting in a shorter life on alternating-current circuits, occured by the "offsetting" of the tantalum wire in the lamp, after long use.

The tantalum lamp was invented, developed and manufactured in Germany, it was introduced in this country, and used here for some years in very large quantities. It was manufactured in this country, but from materials imported from Germany, and complete manufacture was never established here, as at that time the possibilities of the tungsten lamp already loomed up so strongly, that it did not appear economical to develop the manufacture of the tantalum lamp further than necessary to make it available as an intermediate step.

Finally then came the tungsten lamp, or wolfram lamp.[1]

[1] The chemical name of the metal is wolfram; "tungsten," meaning "heavy stone," is merely the name of one of its ores, which in this country has mistakenly been applied to the metal

While the metallized carbon filament (2.5 watts per candle) was exclusively an American development, and the Nernst lamp (1.5 to 2 5 watts per candle), the osmium lamp (1.5 watts per candle) and the tantalum (2 watts per candle) were German developments, merely introduced and adopted in our country, in the development of the tungsten lamp America and Germany have about equally shared.

Originally, tungsten did not appear to be ductile, and ductile tungsten was produced only as the result of extensive research and development, for years therefore, the tungsten filaments were made by some squirting process, just as the osmium and the carbon filaments had been made. One process consisted in squirting the filament of tungsten oxide, then reducing it, and purifying by electrically heating in moist hydrogen Another process squirted the filament of colloidal metallic tungsten; a third process—which appeared specially adaptable to larger filaments, due to the low shrinkage—used a mixture or alloy of finely powdered tungsten with several other metals of successively lower melting and boiling points, squirting such an alloy filament, and then successively driving off the alloying metals by electrically heating.

Finally the research laboratory of the G. E Co. developed ductile tungsten, and with this, all methods of squirting naturally disappeared, and the tungsten lamp or "mazda lamp," as it is usually called by its trade name, is made from drawn tungsten wire, which is wound up on a framework, similar as was done with the tantalum lamp.

As the resistance of tungsten is very much lower than that of carbon, and the power consumption, at the same candlepower, much less, due to its higher efficiency, it follows that the tungsten filament must be very much smaller and longer than the carbon filament of the old

lamp. Great difficulties were thus met with smaller units
of lamp, and with higher voltage as 220, and during the
days of squirted filaments, a number of filaments had to be
used in series in the lamp This naturally increased the
cost of the lamp. The tungsten lamp thus could be
brought down to a reasonable price, made competitive with
the carbon lamp and the question of free lamp renewals
approached, only after the solution of the problem of
ductile tungsten.

The tungsten lamp first appeared with an efficiency of
$1\frac{1}{4}$ to $1\frac{1}{2}$ watts per candlepower, by gradual improvement
in the manufacture of the filament and in the vacuum, the
efficiency was raised to 1 watt per candlepower, and
finally, by the introduction into the lamp bulb of certain
neutral gases of low heat capacity, at partial pressure, in
the so-called "gas-filled mazda lamp" still much higher
efficiencies were made available, reaching in larger units
o 5 and even o 45 watts per candle

With these efficiencies, the tungsten lamp had become
superior not only to all other forms of incandescent lamps,
but also more efficient than any arc lamp, with exception
of the large units of flame arcs and the luminous arcs
As neither of the latter is suitable for indoor illumination,
the use of the arc for indoor illumination thus has entirely
ceased, and the mazda lamp holds sway undisputed in all
indoor lighting

The large unit of the open yellow-flame lamp, of the
short-burning type, is still superior in efficiency to the
large mazda lamp, but unsuited for the conditions of our
country due to the required daily trimming, and the long-
burning yellow-flame arc does not show sufficient superiority in efficiency, which would compensate for its lesser
steadiness, and reliability, and greater complication of

operation, while the white-flame arc lamp usually is inferior in efficiency.

There is left then as the only remaining competitor of the
mazda lamp in outdoor lighting, the luminous arc or
magnetite lamp   This, while about of the same efficiency
as the large mazda lamp, has the disadvantage of being
somewhat less simple in operation, requiring a constant
direct-current circuit, but it has the advantage of perfectly
white light, while even the gas-filled mazda lamp, though
the whitest of all the incandescent lamps, is still decidedly
yellow—so much so, that to make it white by absorbing
the excess of the yellow and red rays in colored glasses,
requires a sacrifice of nearly 75 per cent of the light, that
is, lowers the efficiency to about 2 watts per candle.   For
many purposes, the yellowish-white of the mazda lamp is
no disadvantage, for some purposes it even is an advantage,
it is, however, a serious disadvantage artistically in the
use of the mazda lamp for suburban street lighting, park
lighting and in general, wherever foliage is plentiful,
as the yellowish light gives the green foliage a faded
yellowish look, and thereby spoils its appearance, while
this is not the case with the clear white light of the luminous
arc.

It appears, therefore, that the white luminous arcs
(magnetite, titanium) are the only illuminants, which have
characteristics in efficiency and color value, that assure
their survival in competition with the mazda lamp, in
outdoor illumination

Ductile tungsten, as used in the modern tungsten or
wolfram or mazda lamp, is an extremely interesting material.
It is the heaviest of all known substances, is very hard and
extremely tough, can be drawn out into very small wires,
so small that several dozen of them together are thinner than

a human hair, and fine-drawn wire tungsten is the strongest of all known substances: on thin tungsten wires, tensile strength of over 400,000 lb. per square inch has been observed, which is several times as strong as the strongest steel.

It is interesting to review the various lamp filament materials: now, with our present knowledge, it appears fairly obvious, which might be suitable as filaments, and which not. Especially so with tungsten: tungsten is not a rare and little-known metal, but is extensively used in the industries since a long time. As alloying material in steel, it gives hardness and toughness and special magnetic qualities, which led to its use in magnet steels, while the salts of tungsten have been and are used very extensively for fireproofing inflammable fabrics, as theater decorations. As filament material it had been considered in the early days, but failed by too low a melting point, due to lack of purity. it required the highest chemical art to produce tungsten so pure as to give the required extremely high melting point, as already an extremely small quantity of foreign material as carbon, destroys its usefulness For instance, tungsten carbide is relatively very fusible, and an addition of 1 per cent. of tungsten carbide, to the metallic tungsten, would seriously lower its melting point However, tungsten carbide, CW_2, consists of 96.9 per cent. tungsten and 3.1 per cent. carbon, and the presence of 0 03 per cent. of carbon in the tungsten metal, would already give a contamination of 1 per cent. of carbide, and thereby affect its properties unfavorably.

If all the chemical elements are arranged in order of their atomic weights in a table, they give the so-called "periodic system of elements," that is, all the characteristic properties of the elements are represented by their arrangement in this table. We find then two points or "poles" of volatility, opposite each other, one, at helium and hydrogen, non-metallic elements, and the other one, at mercury, metallic elements. Opposite to each other and to the poles of volatility, we find two poles of refactoriness   the non-metallic pole, at carbon—surrounded by boron, silicon, etc.—and the metallic pole, at .tantalum, tungsten, osmium, iridium.

The choice of filament material thus limits itself to these two points in the system of elements   carbon and its immediately adjacent elements, and tungsten and its immediately adjacent metals.[1]

Of all the elements, carbon is the most refractory, with a melting point probably above 4000°C. Tungsten is next, melting at 3400°C. Thus on first sight we should expect that carbon, with its higher melting point than tungsten, should give a higher efficiency of incandescence, by permitting operation at higher temperature. So it would be, if carbon could be operated as near to its melting point as tungsten. This, however, is not the case, and the melting point alone does not determine the permissible operating temperature of the lamp filament, but the evaporation of the material below the melting point is equally determining

All materials evaporate already below their boiling points, and even below their melting point   Thus ice and snow gradually evaporate. Now with some materials, as tungsten, evaporation below the melting point is very small, so that the temperature can be raised very close

---

[1] It is interesting to note that the melting point rises from the relatively low one of platinum, to iridium and still higher osmium, and on the other side rises from tantalum to tungsten, as the highest   A still higher melting point thust might be expected from the unknown element which fills the gap between tungsten and osmium, the second higher homologue of manganese, if it exists, and this should be superior even to tungsten, as lamp filament

to the melting point, within a few hundred degrees, before appreciable evaporation occurs. Other materials again evaporate very materially even considerably below the melting point, such as camphor for instance Carbon belongs in the latter class, and though its melting point is above 4000°C at 2000°C carbon evaporates already more than tungsten—with its lower melting point, at 3400°C — evaporates at 3000°C. As the carbon vapor deposits on the glass bulb, and, carbon being black, blackens the bulb, and the loss of material reduces the size of the carbon filament, the high rate of evaporation of carbon at temperatures far below the melting and boiling points, thus limits the permissible operating temperature and thereby the available efficiency of the carbon filament to much lower values than given by metals, which, though they melt at lower temperature than carbon, have a much lower evaporation or vapor tension

The reason may probably be found in the size of the atom: carbon has the atomic weight 12, tantalum, tungsten and osmium the atomic weights 185, 187 and 191, and the light carbon atom might be expected to separate from the structure far easier than the metal atom of a weight more than 15 times as heavy.

This also explains the great differences in filament efficiencies, found with different modifications of carbon: the very dense and solid metallic carbon of the gem lamp naturally may be expected to evaporate less, at the same temperature, than the porous and amorphous carbon of the base filament, and with the same evaporation and thereby same lamp life, the former thus could be operated at materially higher temperature and thereby efficiency of light production

The foremost advantage of the metals as filament materials in incandescent lamps, which made the great increase of efficiency of light production possible, thus is not the higher melting point of the metals, but is the low vapor tension of these heavy metals close up to the melting point, which made it possible to take advantage in the operating temperature of the high melting points, while with carbon the high vapor tension at relatively low temperature made it impossible to take advantage of the high melting point

As the evaporation increases with decreasing gas pressure in the lamp bulb, apparently the use of a vacuum should be a disadvantage, and the filament evaporates less, that is, lasts longer or permits higher operating temperature and thus higher radiation efficiency, if operated under considerable gas pressure. With the filament operating in a perfect vacuum, all the electric power put into the lamp is radiated from the filament as visible or invisible light (ultrared radiation), and the higher the temperature, the greater is the radiation efficiency, that is, percentage of visible rays, and therefore also the efficiency of the lamp   If, however, now the lamp bulb is filled with a gas, with the same electric power supplied to it, the temperature of the filament is very greatly lowered, as a large part of the energy is conducted away by the gas, and carried away by gas currents.   To maintain the same filament temperature and thereby the same light production, more energy therefore is required in the gas-filled lamp, than in the vacuum lamp, and the former thus has less efficiency, at the same filament temperature.   However, the reduction of filament evaporation by the gas pressure permits increasing the filament temperature—by still further increasing the power supply—and thereby increasing the radiation-efficiency, that is, the percentage of radiation, which is visible as light, and thus useful, and the question then is, which of the two effects predominates: the loss of efficiency by the waste of energy by convection and conduction by the gas, or the gain in efficiency, by the possibility of operating the filament at a higher temperature.

The loss of energy in the gas depends on the size of the gas-washed filament surface, compared with its volume, and in small lamp units, due to the relatively large filament surface, gas filling offers no advantage, but rather materially lowers the efficiency. In larger units, however, of 100, 300 and 500 watts, the use of a thick filament, coiled in a spiral in a small space, has made it possible to reduce the loss of heat from the filament surface, by convection and conduction through the gas, so much, that the increased operating temperature of the filament gives a substantial increase of efficiency, and in this manner it has been possible in the last years, to more than double the efficiency of light production in the larger lamp units, in the so-called "gas-filled mazda lamp." Most advantageous obviously is a gas of the lowest heat conduction and heat capacity, as nitrogen or argon, while hydrogen for instance, with its high heat conductivity and high specific heat, is harmful under all conditions. The amount of gas is such as to give approximately atmospheric pressure at the operating temperature of the lamp, as safest.

In discussing efficiencies, it must be realized that the incandescent lamp inherently has no definite efficiency, but its efficiency varies with the power supply, or with the impressed voltage, and can be made almost anything.

Thus for instance a mazda lamp, at 25 watts power input, 110 volts, may give 25 candles, that is, an efficiency of 1 watt per candle.

But if we put 35 watts into this lamp, by raising the

voltage to 130, we get 70 candles, or twice the previous efficiency, ½ watt per candle, and if we lower the power supply to 20 watts, by lowering the voltage to 100, we get only 10 candles, corresponding to an efficiency of 2 watts per candle.

However, at 1 watt per candle, the lamp will last an average of 1000 hours, while at the higher efficiency of ½ watt per candle it would last only about 100 hours, and at the lower efficiency of 2 watts per candle will probably last 5000 hours.

Thus, the "efficiency" of an incandescent lamp has a meaning only when related to its life, and any efficiency can be secured by sacrificing the life. Inventors have not always realized this, and so have deceived themselves in believing that they had discovered a wonderful improvement, by forgetting the essential influence of the life on the efficiency

The purpose of the lamp is to give light, and the lamp thus will operate at its highest efficiency, when producing the light at the lowest cost per candle-hour

The cost of light production by the incandescent lamp, per candle-hour, consists of the cost of power and the cost of lamp renewal. Increasing the voltage, decreases the cost of power, but shortens the life and thereby increases the cost of renewal, per lamp-hour, and the reverse is the case with a decrease of voltage. There must thus be a compromise between cost of power and cost of renewal, at which the total cost is a minimum, that is, the economic efficiency of the lamp a maximum.

Supposing 'at 110-volt supply, a mazda lamp consumes 25 watts, gives 25 candles, or 1 watt per candle, and has a life of 1000 hours. Its total light output then is 25,000 candle-hours. It consumes during its life 25 kilowatt-hours and at a cost of 8 cents per kilowatt-hour, and 50 cents per lamp renewal, the total cost of the light given by the lamp would be $25 \times 8 + 50 = \$2\ 50$, that is, 10 cents per 1000 candle-hours.

Suppose now we operate this lamp at 130 volts. Then it consumes 35 watts, gives 70 candles, or ½ watt per candle, but lasts only 100 hours. Its total light output thus is only 7000 candle-hours. The total power consumption is 3 5 kilowatt-hours hence the total cost of operation $3\ 5 \times 8 + 50 = 78$ cents, or 11 4 cents per 1000 candle-hours. That is, though we have doubled the efficiency of light production of the lamp, the cost of the light per lamp-hour has increased, by the decreased length of lamp life

Suppose now we operate this lamp at 100 volts. Then it consumes 20 watts, gives 10 candle, or 2 watts per candle, but lasts 5000 hours. The total light output then is 50,000 candle-hours. The total cost of operation is $100 \times 8 + 50 = \$8\ 50$, or 17 cents per 1000 candle-hours, that is, a materially higher price for the light, showing that it would be very uneconomical to operate the lamp at such low rating, as to give a very long life.

With different costs of power, and different renewal costs, obviously somewhat different results are derived regarding to the most efficient industrial life and the proper efficiency of operation However, as industrial conditions do not vary over such a great range, and such efficiency-life curves are fairly flat, it is possible to strike an average which fairly well satisfies average industrial conditions of the use of the incandescent lamp. If then we speak of the efficiency of an incandescent lamp, we always mean, or should mean, the industrial efficiency, that is, the efficiency which giving minimum cost per candle-hour, considering cost of power as well as cost of renewal.

With the carbon-filament lamp, this problem of lamp efficiency had been studied for many years, and found that a useful life of 500 hours is the most efficient, that is, under the "efficiency" of a carbon-filament incandescent lamp always was understood the efficiency which give to the lamp an average life of 500 hours at 500 hours, the lamp either was burned out, or by blackening of the bulb the efficiency so much lowered as to make the lamp of no further use. This latter maximum permissible decrease of efficiency during useful life had been fixed, by similar consideration, as 20 per cent that is, burn out or decrease of light production to 80 per cent. of the initial terminated the useful life of the carbon lamp.

Incidentally, it is of interest to notice, that blackening of the bulb as cause of gradual deterioration has practically disappeared in the metal-filament lamp, and already had largely decreased in the metallized carbon or gem lamp. these lamps usually end their life either by burn out of the filament, or by impairment of the vacuum, and in the latter case, blackening of the bulb occurs in a few hours, terminating the life, but the gradual blackening, through hundreds of hours, is absent.

As the power consumption of the mazda lamp is less, the cost of renewal somewhat higher, the same consideration of the proper useful life, in relation to the efficiency, which give 500 hours with the carbon lamp, have led to the requirement of a useful life of 1000 hours with the mazda lamp, and 1500 hours with the series street-lighting mazda lamp, and these values seem to very fairly satisfy the industrial conditions.

Obviously, where the cost of power, etc , is very different, materially different conclusions regarding the proper useful life result. This for instance is the case with the small mazda lamps used in pocket flash lights. In these, the power is derived from dry cells, at a cost which probably is between $10 and $50 per kilowatt-hour. At this enormous power cost, even with the small lamp unit and therefore small power consumption, the industrial efficiency maximum lies at a useful life of a few hours only, that is, it is more economical to save power by running the lamp at very high efficiency.

Similar considerations apply also to automobile lamps, kinematoscope lamps, etc, in which a materially shorter industrial life than 1000 hours is economical.

As regards to the meaning of candlepower, for many years, during the days of the carbon filament, a somewhat fictitious rating was used, by a "horizontal candlepower," which was only about 80 per cent of the true, average or mean spherical candlepower, that is, the candlepower which characterizes the total flux of light given by the lamp. The ratio of the nominal or horizontal candlepower, to the true or mean spherical, was then measured and called the "spherical reduction factor," and usually varied between 0.77 and 0 82.

However, with the general introduction of the metal-filament lamp—in which very often the spherical reduction factor is practically unity, that is, the horizontal candlepower equal to the mean spherical—the use of the term horizontal candlepower is rapidly disappearing. Furthermore, a lamp rating in watts is becoming more customary.

SEVENTEENTH LECTURE

ARC LIGHTING

While incandescent lamps can be operated on constant potential as well as on constant current, the arc is essentially a constant-current phenomenon At constant length, the voltage consumed by the arc decreases with increase of current, as shown by curve I in Fig 47. If, therefore, an attempt is made to operate such an arc on constant potential, for instance on 80 volts—which would correspond to 3 9 amperes on curve I—then any tendency of the current to increase—as by a momentary drop of the arc resistance—would lower the required arc voltage, and so increase the current, at constant supply voltage, hence still further lower the arc voltage, etc , and a short-circuit would result. *Vice versa*, a momentary decrease of arc current, by requiring more voltage than is available, would still further decrease the current, increase the required voltage, etc., and the arc would extinguish

Therefore only such apparatus is operative on constant potential, in which an increase of current requires an increase of voltage, and *vice versa;* and so limits itself.

While, therefore, arcs can be operated on a constant-current system, to run arc lamps on constant potential, some current-limiting device is necessary in series with the arc, as a resistance; or, in an alternating-current circuit, a reactance.

The supply voltage required to operate the arc consuming the voltage represented by curve I must therefore be higher than that given by this voltage, and must be at least as

198

high as that given by the curve II. The latter thus is
called the stability curve of the arc. Thus, for instance,
at 4 amperes, the arc cannot be operated at less than 104
volts supply. At 104 volts supply the limit of stability

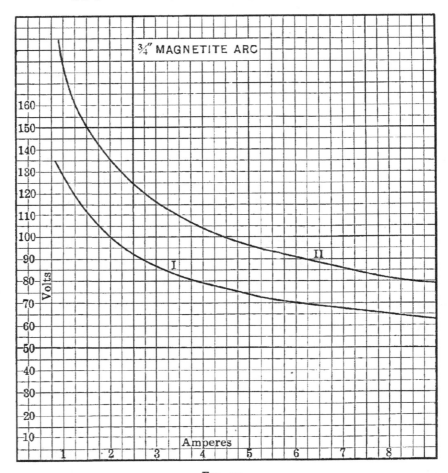

FIG. 47.

is reached; and for supply voltages higher than 104, the
arc is stable, the more so, the higher the supply voltage
is above 104. The difference in voltage between the supply
voltage and the arc voltage is consumed by the "steadying
resistance" of the arc.

High reactance in series with the direct-current arc retards the current fluctuations and so reduces them; so that with reactance in series to the direct-current arc, the arc can be operated by a supply voltage closer to the stability curve II than without reactance; reactance therefore is very essential in the steadying resistance of a direct-current arc. Obviously, no series reactance can enable operation of the arc I on a supply voltage below that given by the stability curve II

Constant-potential arc lamps are, therefore, necessarily less efficient than constant-current arc lamps, due to the power consumed in the steadying resistance. A large part of this power is saved in alternating constant-potential arc lamps, by using reactance instead of resistance, but the power factor is therefore greatly lowered, and the constant-potential alternating arc lamp rarely has a power factor of over 70 per cent.

Where therefore high-potential constant-current circuits are permissible, as for outdoor or street lighting, arc lamps are usually operated on a constant-current circuit, with series connection of from 50 to 100 lamps on one circuit. With the exception of a few of the larger cities, all the street lighting by arc lamps in this country is done by constant-current systems, either direct current or alternating current.

For direct constant-current supply, arc-light machines have been built, and a few, of the Brush type, are still used. In these machines, inherent regulation for constant current is produced by using a very high armature reaction and relatively weak field excitation; that is, the armature ampere-turns are nearly equal and opposite to the field ampere-turns, and thus both very large compared with the difference, the resultant ampere-turns, which produce the magnetic field   A moderate increase of current and consequent increase of armature ampere-turns therefore greatly reduces the resultant ampere-turns and so the field magnetism and the voltage, that is, the machine tends to regulate for constant current.   Perfect constant-current regulation then is secured by some governing device, as an automatic regulator varying a resistance shunted across the series field.   It must, however, be understood that the "regulator" of the arc machine does not give a constant-current regulation, but the armature reaction of the machine does this, and the regulator merely makes it perfect; but even with the regulator disconnected, arc machines give fairly close constant-current regulation.

With the development of the mercury-arc rectifier, which converts constant alternating current into constant direct current, arc machines have gone out of use, as the mercury-arc rectifier in combination with the stationary constant-current transformer enables us to derive constant direct current from the alternating-current constant-potential supply system, without moving machinery.

Constant alternating current is derived by a constant-current transformer or constant-current reactance.   Diagrammatically, the constant-current transformer is shown in Fig. 48.   The primary coil P and the secondary coil S are movable with regard to each other (which of the two coils is movable, is immaterial, or rather, is determined by consideration of design).   Fig 48 shows the coil S suspended and its weight partially balanced by counterweight W.

With the secondary coil S close to the coil P, that is, in the lowest position, most of the magnetism produced by the primary coil P passes through the secondary coil S, and the secondary voltage therefore is a maximum   The further the secondary coil moves away from the primary coil,

the more of the magnetism passes between the coils, the less
through the secondary coil, and the lower therefore is the
secondary voltage, which becomes a minimum (or zero, if
so desired), with the secondary coil at a maximum distance from the primary, that is, in the top position.

Primary current and secondary current are proportional
and in opposition to each other, and repel each other, and
the repulsion is proportional to the product of the two
currents; that is, proportional to the square of the secondary

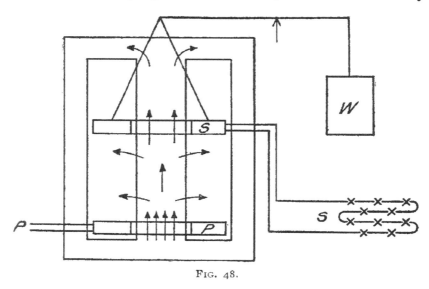

FIG. 48.

current. The weight of the secondary coil is balanced by
the counterweight W and the repulsion from the primary
coil, at normal secondary current. Any increase of secondary current by a decrease of load, increases the repulsion,
in this way pushing the secondary coil further away from
the primary and thereby reducing the secondary voltage
and thus the current; and *vice versa*, a decrease of secondary
current, by an increase of load, reduces the repulsion and
so causes the secondary coil to come nearer to the primary,
that is, increases its voltage and so restores the current.

Such an arrangement regulates for constant current between the voltage limits given by the two extreme positions of the movable coil. These usually are chosen from some margin above full load, down to about one-third load

The constant-current reactance operates on the same principle: the two coils P and S are connected in series with each other into the arc circuit supplied from the constant-potential source, and by separating or coming together, vary in reactance with the load, and thereby maintain constant current

While the alternating-current arc lamp is less efficient, that is, gives less light for the same power, than the direct-current arc lamp, the disadvantages of the use of numerous arc machines had led to the extended adoption of alternating-current series arc lighting before the development of the mercury-arc rectifier, which enabled the operation of direct-current arc circuits from constant-current transformers. Thousands of such enclosed series alternating arc lamps are still in use all over the country, though they have long ceased to have any right of existing, as they are very much inferior in efficiency to the luminous arc or magnetite, and to the mazda incandescent lamp: the latter giving three or more times as much light for the same power consumption.

The carbon arc lamp of old has for over a generation dominated all outdoor or street lighting, and much of the indoor lighting indeed practically all lighting of larger areas, as halls, assembly places, etc. It originated even before the carbon-filament incandescent lamp, represented a much larger unit of light, and gave a much higher efficiency, so that during the days of the carbon-filament incandescent lamp, wherever a large unit of light could be used, the arc lamp found its proper field. By the metal-filament incandescent lamp, and especially the mazda lamp, the plain carbon arc lamp has, however, become outclassed so enormously, that it is only a historical curiosity today

In the plain carbon arc lamp practically all light comes from the incandescent tips of the carbons, very little from the arc flame.   Once more, then, by using materials in the arc-lamp electrodes, which in the arc flame give an intensely luminous spectrum, the arc lamp was made competitive with the newer metal-filament incandescent lamps, by adding the large amount of light given by the luminous arc flame, and so greatly increasing the efficiency of the arc lamp in the flame arc lamp and the luminous arc lamp.

So far only three materials have been found, which in luminous arcs give efficiencies vastly superior to incandescence: mercury, calcium (lime), and titanium.

The mercury arc has the advantage of perfect steadiness, a long life—requiring no attention for thousands of hours— and high efficiency over a fairly wide range of candlepowers; but it is seriously handicapped for many purposes by its bluish-green color.

In the flame carbon lamp carbons impregnated with calcium compounds, usually calcium fluoride, borate, etc., are used, and the arc then has an orange-yellow color. The compounds, after coloring the arc and giving it efficiency, escape as smoke, the arc therefore must be an open arc, or provisions made to condense and collect the deposit.

The open arc lamp, which was used in the early days, had, however, been almost entirely superseded by the enclosed carbon arc, in spite of the somewhat lower efficiency of the latter; and the inconvenience of daily attendance required by an open arc, and the large consumption of carbons, makes a return to this type impracticable.   For this reason the open-flame carbon lamp has not proven suitable for general outdoor illumination, as street lighting.

Enclosed-flame carbon arc lamps thus were designed, in which by a circulating system between a double set of glass globes the smoke is deposited at some place where it does not obstruct the light, and such "long burning," or "enclosed" or "regenerative" flame carbon lamps, with yellow color of light, have been fairly successful and found an extensive introduction in street lighting. But in efficiency they were somewhat inferior to the open or short-burning flame arc, and thus, when the gas-filled mazda lamp entered the field with $\frac{1}{2}$ watt efficiency, or better, whatever little superiority in efficiency may still have existed in the large-flame arc, did not appear sufficient to compensate for the lesser steadiness and greater complication of operation, and thus the enclosed yellow-flame lamp is rapidly going out of use, in competition with the gas-filled mazda lamp. The white-flame carbon arc always has been inferior in efficiency to the yellow-flame, and thus has never found an extensive use on the basis of efficiency competition, but has merely been used to a limited extent, due to its color value, and in this respect it has never made much headway against the luminous arc or magnetite lamp, which in steadiness, efficiency and constancy of the color is superior to the white-flame carbon lamp.

The only type of arc lamp, which thus has been able to hold and extend its field against the competition of the mazda incandescent lamp, is the luminous arc, in which carbon has entirely been eliminated from the electrodes, and the light-giving electrode consists of the oxides of iron, titanium and chromium, with small quantities of alkali fluorides as steadier of the arc flame: the intermediate oxide of iron, magnetite, is the arc conductor, and composes the major part of the electrode. The oxide of titanium—rutile—is the light-giver, therefore used in as large a percentage as practicable without interfering with steadiness and conductivity, and the oxide of chromium, used in a lesser percentage, is the steadier or restrainer it increases the steadiness of the flame, and increases the life of the electrode, thus giving electrode life of 150 to 300 hours However, in too large percentage, chromium again lowers the efficiency, and its use is thereby limited.

In commercial efficiency, the luminous arc is about equal to the highest efficiencies of the gas-filled mazda lamp; in operation it is cheaper as regards to the renewal of electrodes, but as arc lamp, on a constant direct-current system through mercury-arc rectifiers, it is somewhat more complicated, requiring more attention than the operation of gas-filled mazdas on a constant-potential series system. In color, however, the luminous arc is perfectly white, and therefore has the advantage wherever foliage, trees and plants are within the rays of the light, and their appearance is of interest, as the luminous arc does not give the faded and dead look to foliage, which the yellow carbon arc as well as the yellow incandescent lamp, even still the gas-filled mazda lamp, gives It, therefore, appears, that both types of outdoor illuminants, the mazda incandescent lamp and the magnetite arc lamp, will retain legitimate fields of application, while for all indoor illumination, the mazda lamp entirely covers the field. The development of an alternating-current luminous arc lamp, that is, a lamp which could be operated directly from a constant alternating-current circuit without rectifier, would still further extend the field of the luminous arc in outdoor illumination, if of competitive efficiency, and such a lamp probably will sometime make its appearance.

In the arc lamp, the current is carried across the gap
between the terminals by a stream of vapor of the electrodes;
thus the electrodes consume more or less rapidly. Some
feeding mechanism is therefore required to move the electrodes toward each other during their consumption This
arc lamp mechanism may be operated by the current, or
by the voltage, or by both. This gives the three different
types of lamps· the series lamp, the shunt lamp, and the
differential lamp.

In the series lamp, an electromagnet energized by the
lamp current, and balanced against a weight or a spring,
moves the carbons toward each other when by their
burning off, the arc lengthens and the current decreases.
Obviously, this lamp cannot be used on constant-current
circuits, or with several lamps in series, but only as single
lamp on constant-potential circuits.

In the shunt lamp, the controlling magnet is shunted
across the arc, and with increasing arc length and consequent arc voltage, moves the electrodes toward each
other. In constant-current circuits, this lamp tends toward hunting, and therefore requires a very high reactance
in series; it thereby gives a lower power factor in alternating-
current circuits, and has therefore been superseded by the
differential lamp. It has, however, the advantage of not
being sensitive to changes of current.

In the differential lamp, an electromagnet in series with
the arc opposes an electromagnet in shunt to the arc, and
the lamp regulates for constant arc resistance. It was the
lamp most universally used in constant-potential and
constant-current systems, as most stable in its operation;
but in constant-current systems, it requires that the current
be constant within close limits· if the current is low, the
arc is too short, and the lamp gives very little light, and

if the current is high, the arc becomes so long as to endanger the lamp

From the operating mechanism the motion is usually transmitted to the electrode by a clutch, which releases and lets the electrodes slip together.

In the carbon arc lamp of old, the mechanism was "floating;" that is, the upper carbon, held by the opposing forces of shunt and series magnets, moves with every variation of the arc resistance, and so maintains very closely constant voltage on the arc. In the long-burning luminous arc, as the magnetite lamp, the light comes from the arc flame, and thus constant length of arc flame is required for constant light production. The floating mechanism, which constantly varies the arc length with the variation of the arc resistance, has therefore been superseded by a mechanism which sets the arc at fixed length, and leaves it there until with the consumption of the electrodes the arc has sufficiently lengthened to cause the shunt coil to operate and to reset the arc length. Thus in some respects, these lamps are shunt lamps

During the early days of the open carbon arc lamp, 9 6, 6.6 and 4 amperes were the currents used in direct-current arc circuits, with about 40 volts per lamp. The 4-ampere arc very soon disappeared, as giving practically no light

In the enclosed arc lamp, the carbons are surrounded by a nearly air-tight globe, which restricts the admission of air and thus the combustion of the carbon, and so increases the life of the carbons from 8 or 10 hours to 70 to 120 hours. In these lamps, lower currents and higher arc voltages, that is, longer arcs, are used in direct-current circuits, 6 6 amperes and 5 amperes, with 70 to 75 volts per lamp; in alternating-current circuits, 7.5 and 6.6 amperes are used with the same arc voltage

In the direct-current magnetite arc lamp, 4 amperes, 6.6 amperes and sometimes 5 amperes, and 75 to 80 volts per lamp are used.

In the application to outdoor lighting, both types of lamps, the luminous arc and the mazda incandescent, can obviously be applied in the same manner: either, in the usual form of street lighting, as fairly large units, 250 to 500 watts, on high poles and with considerable spacing along the sides of the street, or where trees abound, preferably in the middle of the street, or, in so-called ornamental lighting, on ornamental standards, with underground cable supply, along the two sides of the street in business thoroughfares, as so-called "white way lighting," or in smaller units in so-called "ornamental" or "boulevard lighting," in the middle of the boulevard in grass and flower plots. In the latter case, the mazda lamp has the advantage that more frequent smaller units can be used, while the ornamental magnetite lamp, with 300 watt power consumption, requires a wider spacing, but on the other hand by its white color of light gives a better appearance of the lawns, trees and foliage in general.

EIGHTEENTH LECTURE

MODERN POWER GENERATION
AND DISTRIBUTION

With the development of electrical engineering, electricity is more and more becoming the universal form
of power, supplying the energy demand of modern civilization, and the various local power stations, electric
generating stations, etc , are rapidly being replaced by
substations, receiving the power from huge electric generating stations or groups of such stations, over a system of
high-power feeders, and converting it into whatever form
of energy is demanded · electrical, mechanical, chemical, etc.

Thus power generation has become a separate industry,
distinct from the use of power.

In these huge electric power stations, of hundred thousands of kilowatt capacity, experience has shown three
features as essential for successful operation

1 All electrical apparatus must be operated in parallel
on the same set of busbars, not only the generators in one
station, but where a number of stations feed into the same
system, they must operate in parallel over tie cables,
thereby essentially giving one set of busbars, interconnecting all the generating stations, as a ring bus—as shown diagrammatically by the heavy black lines in Fig. 50.   Where
two frequencies are used, on the generators, as 60 and 25
cycles, they are preferably synchronized with each other
through frequency changers,·to secure the interchange of
power between them.

210

2. The generating system must be capable of unlimited expansion, by extension of the power houses or the joining into the system of additional power houses, without any increase of the risk and danger of operation, that is, without reducing the reliability of operation or increasing the chances for trouble. Therefore

3 The control of the system must be such that the maximum amount of power, which can be let loose destructively in case of accident, at any point of the system, is not increased by an increase of the size of the system, and is limited to a value, which can under emergency condition safely be handled and controlled by modern circuit-opening and controlling devices.

I in Fig 49 shows diagrammatically an arrangement of such high-power stations, containing six generators, G_1 to G_6.

The generators usually are high-voltage three-phase turbo-alternators, of 10,000 to 50,000 kilowatt capacity, feeding directly into the power distribution feeders at about 10,000 volts (6000 to 15,000 volts) In the larger units of steam-turbine alternators, such very high efficiencies have been reached on the electrical as well as on the steam end, that there appears very little probability, at least for a long time to come, that any form of internal combustion engine should approach the efficiencies of steam-turbine electric power generation, and the steam turbine thus has become the universal source of primary power, and will undoubtedly remain it for the next future.

Assuming the generators G in Fig 49 to be 20,000 kilowatt units. In case of accidental short-circuit at the generator terminals, the only limitation of the momentary short-circuit current is the internal self-inductive reactance of the generator, usually of about 3 to 4 per cent in turbo-alternators. That is, at the rated current, the internal reactance consumes 3 to 4 per cent. of the rated voltage, and at short-circuit current, where the total machine voltage is—in the first instance, that is, before armature

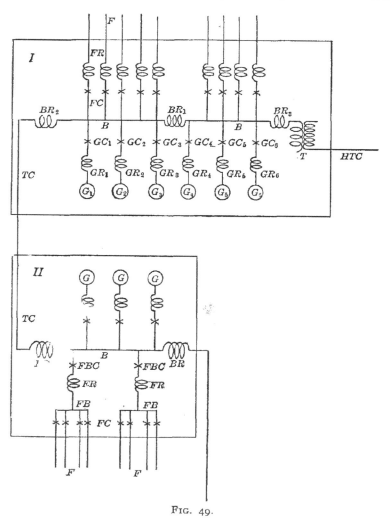

FIG. 49.

reaction comes into play—consumed by the self-inductive reactance, the short-circuit·current would thus be 33 to 25 times the rated current, and with six generators directly connected to the busbars, a short-circuit at the busbars would let loose a momentary current 200 to 150 times that of one generator, giving a momentary maximum power of 2,000,000 to 1,500,000 kilowatts [1] Obviously, no circuit-breakers or other devices of a size such as to permit their economical use in every generator, can control such enormous power.

The power which the generators can feed into the system is therefore limited by "power-limiting reactances," inserted into the generator leads, as shown in Fig 49 as GR_1 to GR_6.

Fig 49 as diagrammatical representation shows one phase only: obviously three reactances, etc , are required at every generator These generator reactances are treated as a part of the generator, and the generator circuit breakers thus located between the reactances GR and the busbars B.

In general, in large high-power generating systems, the power-limiting generator reactances are chosen so as to limit the momentary (symmetrical) generator short-circuit current to about 10 times the generator current, that is, a total generator reactance of 8 to 12 per cent. is aimed at. Assuming an internal reactance in the generators of 4 per cent., the external reactances GR thus would be designed for 4 to 8 per cent. reactance.

The size of such power-limiting reactances is conveniently expressed in per cent , an 8 per cent. generator power-limiting reactance thus means a reactance having a terminal voltage equal to 8 per cent. of the generator voltage, at the rated generator current.

But even with the maximum short-circuit current of the generators limited by generator reactance GR, with increasing size of the system, and thus increasing number of genera-

---

[1] The maximum power of an alternator may approximately be considered as open-circuit volts times short-circuit current divided by 2.

tors feeding into the busbars, soon conditions are reached giving a destructive accumulation of power at the busbars in case of a short-circuit   Assuming for instance in Fig. 49 three power-house feeding into the busbars, I with 6, II with 3; and III again with six generators of 20,000 kilowatts each, or a total of 300,000 kilowatts—which is less than some existing stations.   With the short-circuit current limited to 10 times the rated current, by the generator reactance, the maximum short-circuit current would correspond to 3,000,000 kilowatts, and the maximum power available at a short at the busbars, might reach 1,500,000 kilowatts, which is beyond the capacity of circuit-controlling devices

Thus a further limitation of power became necessary in these huge systems, by the use of busbars reactances, shown in Fig 49 as BR_1, BR_2, BR_3 That is, the busbar is divided into sections, which are joined by reactances BR. No interference with parallel operation occurs by these busbar reactances—unless they are of excessive reactance—but they limit the power which can be let loose at any busbar section, and thereby permit indefinite increase of the system, without increasing danger from possible accumulation of power.

As each busbar section, B_1, B_2, B_3, etc., receives power from generators, and sends power out into feeders, the flow of power along the busbars, over the busbar reactances BR, is only the difference between the power generated and that consumed in any busbar section, and by reasonable care in choosing the number of generators operating at each busbar section, the exchange of power over the busbar reactances can be kept very moderate theoretically, to less than one-quarter the output of one generator.

It is therefore permissible, and desirable, to choose

higher values in the busbar reactances, than in the generator reactances, and from 20 to 30 per cent reactances are not infrequently used in the busbars

A 20 per cent. reactance would mean, that the potential difference across this reactance, when traversed by the rated current of one generator, is 20 per cent. of the rated voltage. In case of a dead short-circuit on one busbar section, and with full voltage maintained at the adjoining busbar section, the busbar reactances would have to absorb the total voltage, thus, as 20 per cent. reactance, carry 5 times the rated current of a generator, or both busbar reactances together (at either end of the short-circuited busbar section) 10 times the generator current If then each busbar section contains three generators, limited to 10 times their rated current at short-circuit, the maximum short-circuit current of such a busbar section would be that coming from three generators and two busbar reactances, or 40 times the rated current of a generator, giving a maximum possible power development at the busbar, of 400,000 kilowatts. This is within the range of emergency capacity of modern high-power circuit-breakers, thus can be controlled safely—though obviously not without the circuit-breakers showing distress of overload, throwing oil, and requiring cleaning up after the operation

It must be realized that even with considerable current flowing over a busbar reactance, and thus considerable potential difference at the reactor terminals, this does not mean a drop of voltage and thus a voltage difference between adjoining busbar sections As the reactive voltage is in quadrature with the main voltage, it is absorbed by a phase difference between the (equal) voltages of adjoining busbars For instance, even with full rated generator current flowing over a 20 per cent. busbar reactance, the reactive voltage of 20 per cent would be taken care of by the terminal voltages of the adjoining busbar section being out of phase by 20 per cent. that is, displaced in phase by $2 \sin \phi/2 = 0$ 20, or by $12°$, in other words by such a small angle as not to affect the operation regarding stability, etc. This phase displacement obviously would be brought about by increasing the generator excitation in the busbar section which sends out, reducing it in the section which receives power from the adjoining busbar section, adjusting both excitation so as to have the same voltage in both busbar sections.

The use of busbar reactances made it permissible to tie together the various power houses of the system, into one unified system, by tie cables TC and HTC, as shown in Fig. 49 Conveniently, such tie cables between two power houses would be the location of a busbar dividing reactance, BR_2 and BR_3, and if possible, this reactance would be divided in two, and half located at either end of the cable, so as to separate a breakdown of the cable from the busbars.

Obviously, several, two to six or more, cables would as a rule be used in multiple in the tie lines between the stations, and where the distance between the stations is large, as between 1 and 111, step-up transformers T inserted between the tie cable and the station, that is, with 10,000-volt generation and distribution, a 20,000 or 30.000-volt tie line or ring cable used between the stations, to join them together

From the busbar sections then branch off the power feeders F, through their circuit-breakers FC, as diagrammatically shown in Fig, 49.

Reactances in the feeders "feeder reactances," as shown as FC in Fig. 49, are not always used, and are not so essential, since the limitation of the power in the busbars, by generator and busbar reactances, also limits the power in the feeder short-circuit. However, breakdowns in feeders are very much more frequent than in the station, and as a feeder short-circuit close to the generating station is practically at the busbar—if no feeder reactance is used—and the power concentrated in a busbar short-circuit is still very large, it is desirable, and good practice tends more and more to the use of feeder reactances also. Usually somewhat smaller reactances are used, as 4 per cent However, a 4 per cent. feeder reactance means much more reactance than an 8 per cent generator reactance, as the former refers to the current rating of the feeder, which is very much less than that of the generator. Thus a 4 per cent feeder reactance would in general reduce the effect of a short-circuit in the feeder near the generating station, to a small fraction of the jolt which would result without the feeder reactance.

It is obvious that various arrangements and modifications can be made in the size and proportioning, location, etc , of reactances and other controlling elements, fulfilling the same general purpose, and diagram Fig 49 thus is essentially only illustrative Thus for instance, a different arrangement of feeders is shown in station 11 of Fig. 49. groups of feeders joined together on small feeder buses *FB*, and the latter connected to the main bus by feeder reactance *FR* and emergency feeder circuit-breaker *FBC*.

Furthermore, local and industrial limitations, as space and location, etc , may modify the layout of the station, and require serious study to secure the required safety within the local limitations.

As seen, the safety of the system depends entirely on the reliability of the power-limiting reactances: generators may burn out and circuit-breakers fail, without giving more than local trouble, as long as the power-limiting reactances block the extension of the trouble.

Thus the utmost reliability of the power-limiting reactances is of the foremost importance, and they should be the last structural element, where cheapness is considered.

Furthermore, the service of the reactances is specially severe, since it is not under their normal operating conditions, but under abnormal conditions, under enormous overstress, that they are called upon to fulfill their functions of safeguard: under short-circuit, when traversed by ten times their normal current, that is, exposed to 100 times the normal mechanical stresses between the conductors, exposed to 100 times the normal i^2r heating, then their reliability is essential for the system   Also, as inductances interconnected between cables, static discharges and impulses are liable to pick out the reactances, and if once an impulse flashes over between turns and short-circuits, the reactance ceases to be a reactance, fails in its function Thus in the design of such reactance, safety of the systems which are to be protected, requires that every consideration˙ should be given to their utmost reliability. they must contain nothing which might possibly give way, break or get loose even under enormous mechanical overstresses; there must be nothing inflammable or combustible, which might be damaged by heat; there must be no metal or other conductor, whether insulated or grounded, near the circuit of the reactance, to which electrostatic sparks could flash and start a short-circuit between turns, in short they should be the most reliable of all the station parts.

Such power-limiting reactance as a rule must be air reactance, that is, cannot contain an iron core, as the use of the latter would make the reactance uneconomically large, due to the very low magnetic density required in the iron. In a 10 per cent reactance, under short-circuit, that is, under the condition under which the reactance is needed and therefore must be fully there, the magnetic density is ten times the normal, as the current is increased tenfold, and as in the former case the iron must be below magnetic saturation—otherwise the reactor would lose its reactance just when it is needed—it follows that normally a density would have to be used, so low as to be hopelessly uneconomical in iron With a 4 per cent. reactance, this would be still worse, as it would have to operate at less than 4 per cent. of magnetic saturation. This is the reason why in all such power-limiting reactances air cores or the equivalent (concrete cores) are used, and iron excluded.

In general, such high-power generating systems are either 25 cycles or 60 cycles, in the larger systems 25 cycles are usually preferred, but the extensive use of 60 cycles led to the introduction of 60-cycle generators in addition to the 25-cycle ones, so that the modern very high-power generating systems contain 25 cycles and some 60-cycle alternators, with frequency changers interlocking the two systems and providing for interchange of power.

The distribution of power from these huge power-generating stations of Fig. 49, then is shown diagrammatically in Fig. 50.

G_1, G_2 and G_3 show three generating stations, G_1 and G_3 containing six generators each, in two sections divided by a busbar reactance, and G_2 contains one section of three generators, thus a total of fifteen generators in five sections of 60,000 kilowatts rated capacity, each The three stations are joined in a common ring bus, shown in heavy drawn line, consisting of underground cable between the stations: low-tension cable between the adjoining stations G_1 and G_2, and high-tension cable fed through transformers, between the distant station G_3, and the other two stations.

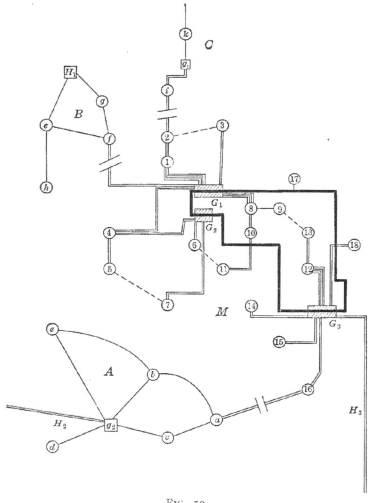

FIG. 50.

From these generating stations are fed a number of substations, denoted by numbers 1 to 20, through power feeders, each substation usually receiving two to four feeders, as shown in Fig. 50. The different feeders of the same substation are preferably derived from different busbar sections or even power houses, to increase the reliability of operation, that is, maintain power on the substation, even if a busbar section or even an entire power house should go out of service As far as possible, however, for convenience of control and reliability of operation, the different substations are fed from separate feeders, so that trouble in one substation is less liable to involve other substations, and troubles in a feeder extends to its substation only However, this is not always economically feasible, and sometimes two or more substations are connected to the same feeders, as shown in Fig. 50. To some extent, substations may be tied together by tie cables, shown dotted in Fig. 50. This is a great economic advantage, in saving cable capacity by permitting interchange of power between substations, but it makes the control of the system far more difficult, especially when carried out to a considerable extent, and no perfectly satisfactory device has yet been developed to overcome this disadvantage.

In the substations, the power supplied from the generating stations then is transformed down to 2200-volt three or four-wire, for general alternating-current distribution for lighting and power, or, if the generating stations are 25 cycles, the power is converted by frequency changers from 25-cycle supply to 60-cycle distribution. Direct-current three-wire converters supply power for three-wire underground Edison direct-current distribution, 600-volt synchronous converters feed railway systems, industrial power, factories and mills are supplied by other substations; in short, these substations 1 to 18 fulfill all the functions of the electrical generating stations of former times, and indeed very often have been generating stations, which, with the erection of the unified high-power central stations, were changed to substations.

In the densely populated "metropolitan" district, M of Fig 50, distribution is essentially by underground cables, at 10,000 volts, more or less, through large substations from which all the power demands of the territory are supplied.

In the less densely populated territory throughout the country, and the State, the distribution more commonly used is overhead, frequently at 30,000-volt isolated delta, as a very convenient voltage, and when well-built and well-insulated, most reliable in operation   Such systems, as shown at A, B and C, then tie into the metropolitan system M by feeders, with transformers located at the place of change from underground to overhead.   The substations, a, b * * * k, then are similar distribution centers as 1, 2 * * * 18 in the metropolitan territory, different only in size and character of load as depending on the local require-ments.   Commonly, they have been generating systems, feeding smaller cities, villages, etc., and often they still contain some of the generating machinery as reserve and for emergency use, or for use during peak loads.

In such outlying feeders and circuits, usually a steam-turbine sustaining station is provided, as shown at g_1, g_2, etc , that is, at one of the larger stations near the end of the circuit, a turbo-alternator of a few thousand kilowatts is installed and controls and sustains voltage and power.

Where water power exists, water-power stations may be included in such network of outlying distribution, as at H_1, and further-distant water powers feed into the system, as at H_2 Also, long-distance water-power lines may tie into the main generating station, as shown at H_3, and these water powers may then be used either for supplying whatever power they may happen to have available. much in spring and fall, possibly nothing in summer, or they may be merely reserve or standby connections, permitting the system to draw power from the water power, when much power is needed, or when an accident has disabled a part of the steam plant, or to supply the customers of the hydraulic plant from the steam-turbine station in case of the failure or deficiency of the hydraulic plant.

It is obvious that a variety of arrangements and methods of installation and operation is feasible, depending on the local conditions, the relative amounts of concentrated metropolitan load and of distributed rural load, etc , in organizing the modern system of general power generation and distribution to substations which take the place of the smaller generating stations of former times, but as part of the huge system, share in the higher economy of power production, of administration and of operation, of the larger unified system

APPENDIX I

EFFECT OF ELECTRICAL ENGINEERING
ON MODERN CIVILIZATION

(From an address before the Franklin Institute, 1914)

I

The use of electricity in modern civilized life is rapidly increasing in lighting our homes, factories, streets; in industrial power applications; in domestic service, from the fan motor to the electric bell or the heating and cooking device, in transportation, while no great inroads have yet been made into the field of the steam locomotive, an entire system of electric railroads has sprung up all over the country, fully comparable in size and power demand with the steam railway system; large new industries have developed in electrochemistry and electrometallurgy, supplying us with materials unavailable before—as aluminum—or improving the production of other materials—as copper refining, etc

All these applications are uses of *energy*   In nearly all, electrical energy is replacing some other form of energy used heretofore: chemical energy of fuel, or mechanical energy of steam or gas engines, etc.

To understand the reasons which enable electrical energy to compete successfully with other forms of energy, which are longer and more familiarly known, we have to look into its characteristics.

Electrical energy can be transported—or, as we usually call it, transmitted—economically over practically any distance. Mechanical energy can be transmitted over a limited distance only, by belt or rope drive, by compressed air, etc., heat energy may be carried from a central steam heating plant for some hundred feet with moderate efficiency, but there are only two forms of energy which can be transmitted over practically any distance—that is, which in the distance of transmission are limited only by the economical consideration of a source of energy nearer at hand electrical energy, and the chemical energy of fuel. These two forms of energy thus are the only competitors whenever energy is required at a place distant from any of Nature's stores of energy Thus, when in the study of a problem of electric power transmission we consider whether it is more economical to transmit power electrically from the water power or the coal mine, or generate the power by a steam plant at the place of demand, both really are transmission problems, and the question is whether it is more economical to carry energy electrically over the transmission line, or to carry it chemically, as coal by the railroad train or boat, from the source of energy supply to the place of energy demand, where the energy is converted into the form required, as into mechanical energy by the electric motor or by steam boiler and engine or turbine

Electrical energy and chemical energy both share the simplicity and economy of transmission or transportation, but electrical energy is vastly superior in the ease, simplicity, and efficiency of conversion into any other form of energy, while the conversion of the chemical energy of fuel into other forms of energy is difficult, requiring complicated plants and skilled attendants, and is so limited in efficiency as to make the chemical energy of fuel unavailable for all but very restricted uses: heating, and the big, high-power steam plant. Pressing the button turns on the electric

light and thereby starts conversion into radiating energy:
with chemical energy as source, either special fuels are
required—in the candle, kerosene lamp—or a complex gas
plant. Closing the switch starts the motor, whether a
small fan motor, or a 1000-horsepower motor supplying the
water system of a city or driving the railroad train. With
fuel as source of energy, boiler plant, steam engine, or
turbine, with its numerous auxiliaries, with skilled attendants, etc., are necessary, and the efficiency is low except in
very large units. To appreciate the complexity of the
conversion of the chemical energy of fuel, compared with
the simplicity of electrical energy conversion, imagine the
domestic fan motor with coal as source of energy a small
steam engine, with boiler and furnace, attached to the fan:
to start the fan, we have to make a coal fire and raise
steam to drive the engine This illustrates how utterly
unavailable the chemical energy of fuel is for general
energy distribution. General energy distribution, therefore, may justly be said to date from the introduction of
electric power.

Equally true is the reverse · the conversion of mechanical
or other energy into electrical is simple and economical, while
the conversion into chemical energy is not. Hence, one
of the two large sources of Nature's energy, the water
power, was, before the days of electrical engineering,
useless except to a very limited extent, since the location
of the water power is rarely such that the energy could be
used at its source. The water powers thus have really
been made available only by the development of electrical
transmission.

Characteristic of electrical energy is that it can be concentrated to an energy density higher than any other form of
energy, and results can thus be produced by it which no

other form of energy can bring about, or things done directly by the brute force of energy, as we may say, which formerly had to be brought about in a roundabout way.

Thus iron can be reduced from its ores by the chemical energy of coal in the blast furnace, but aluminum and calcium cannot, as their chemical affinity is higher, and require the higher energy concentration available with electric power. Iron reduced in the blast furnace combines with carbon to cast iron. So calcium combines with carbon in the electric furnace to carbide, the starting material of acetylene, and of cyanamid and the modern fertilizer industry. Platinum can just be melted, and quartz softened, in the hottest flames of combustion the oxy-acetylene flame and the oxy-hydrogen flame. But in the electric arc platinum and quartz and every existing substance, even tungsten and carbon, can be melted and distilled or sublimed Thus mighty industries have grown up and many new materials made available to man, as aluminum, silicon, calcium, chromium, the carbides, cyanamid, acetylene, etc.; others produced in a cheaper manner, as alkalies, hypochlorites, phosphorus, magnesium, sodium, etc.

Electricity as such is the most useless form of energy: it is not found in Nature in industrially available quantities, and finds no industrial use as electrical energy, but it is always produced from some other form of energy, and converted into some other form of energy: light, mechanical energy, chemical energy, heat, etc That is, electrical energy is entirely the connecting link, the intermediary, by which energy is brought from the place where it is found to the place where it is used, or changed from the form in which it is found to the form in which it is used. Thus, on first sight, it appears a roundabout way, when, for instance, in modern electrical ship propulsion an electric generator is placed on the steam turbine, a motor on the ship propeller, a few feet away, though it is not different from practically every other use of electric energy: a transmission link, superior to any other transmission by the flexibility given by the simplicity and economy of conversion

The most serious disadvantage of electrical energy is that it cannot be stored. It is true, there exists the electric storage battery, and it is used to a large extent as standby battery in high-grade electric distribution systems to give absolute reliability of service, or as battery floating on a railway circuit to equalize fluctuations of power, or in special applications, as electric automobiles It does not really store electrical energy, but stores energy by conversion of the electrical into chemical energy, and reconversion, in discharge, of the chemical into electrical energy.

The economic efficiency of the storage battery—using the term in the broad sense including interest on the plant investment and depreciation—is so low that the storage battery does not come into consideration in the industrial storage of energy—that is, in making the rate of electrical energy consumption independent of that of energy production. We can best realize this by comparing electrical energy with the chemical energy of fuel the latter can be stored with perfect economy. Thus, when using fuel as the source of energy—in a steam plant—no serious difficulty is met by the industry even if the fuel supply is interrupted for months, as in the case of a supply by water, through the closing of the navigation by ice. we would simply bring in a sufficient coal supply to last until the navigation opens again in spring. But with electrical energy from a water power we could never dream of storing energy by storage battery to last over the 2 or 3 months during which the river runs dry and the water power fails.

This means that electrical energy must be consumed at the rate at which it is produced, and the cost of electrical energy thereby becomes dependent on the rate of the energy use   This is not the case with most other forms of energy, as, for instance, the chemical energy of fuel. The price of a ton of coal, as determined by the cost of supplying it, is the same whether I dump the coal into a furnace all at once, or whether I use it up at a uniform rate in a small stove, lasting for weeks   If I consume 2400 cubic feet of gas per day, its cost and thereby its price is the same whether I use the gas at a uniform rate throughout the day, of 100 cubic feet per hour, or whether I use the entire 2400 cubic feet in 1 hour, nothing in the remaining 23 hours· the gas is produced at whatever rate is most economical, stored in the gas holders and supplied from there at whatever rate it is required for consumption   If, however, I use 240 kilowatt-hours of electrical energy per day, it makes a very great difference in the cost of supplying this energy whether I use it at a uniform rate of 10 kilowatt-hours per hour, or whether I use the entire 240 kilowatt-hours in 1 hour, nothing in the remaining 23 hours   In the former case, 10 kilowatts of generating machinery are necessary in the steam or hydraulic station producing the electric energy, 10 kilowatts capacity in transmission lines, transformers, substation and distribution lines, to supply the demand   In the latter case, 240 kilowatts of generating machinery, 240 kilowatts of line and transformer capacity are absorbed, and that part of the cost of supplying the electric energy, which consists of interest in investment in the plant, of depreciation, etc —in short, the fixed cost— is 24 times as high in the latter as in the former case. If the fixed cost approximates half the total cost in a steam plant, or is by far the largest part of the total cost in a hydraulic plant, it follows that in the case of concentrated energy used during a short time the cost of electric energy—and with it the price—will be very much larger— many times, possibly—than in the case of a uniform energy consumption.

Thus, due to the absence of storage, the cost of electrical energy essentially depends on the uniformity of the rate of its use—that is, on the load factor, as the ratio of the average consumption to the maximum consumption.

If I use 240 kilowatt-hours of electrical energy in 1 hour, nothing during the remaining 23 hours, that part of the cost which is the fixed cost of plant investment and depreciation is 24 times as great as if I used the same amount of energy at a uniform rate throughout the day   In the former case, if somebody else uses 240 kilowatt-hours, but during another hour of the day, the same plant supplies his energy, and the fixed cost thus is cut practically in two—that is, the cost of energy to both of us is materially reduced   Thus, again, the cost of electrical energy, and with it its price, depends on the overlap or not overlap of the use of the energy by different users, the so-called "diversity factor." The greater the diversity factor—that is, the less the different uses overlap and the more their combination, therefore, increases the uniformity of the total energy demand, the "station load factor"—the lower is the energy cost   The cost of electrical energy for lighting, where all the demand comes during the same part of the day, is inherently much higher than the cost for uniform 24-hour service in chemical works, and with the increasing variety of load, with the combination of energy supply for all industrial and domestic purposes, the cost of energy decreases

Thus, unlike other forms of energy, due to the absence of energy storage, electrical energy can have no definite cost of production, but, even supplied from the same generating station, its cost varies over a wide range, depending on the load factor of the individual use and the diversity factor of the different uses.

This feature, of necessity, must dominate the economical use of electrical energy in industrial, domestic, and transportation service.

II

Civilization results in the complete interdependence of all members of society upon each other. Amongst the savages each individual, family, or tribe is independent, produces everything it requires. In the barbarian state some barter develops, followed by trade and commerce with increasing civilization. But up to a fair state of civilization—up to nearly 100 years ago—all necessities of life were still produced in the immediate neighborhood of the consumer, each group or territory still independent in its existence, and commerce dealing with such things only which were not absolutely necessary for life. All this has now changed, and in our necessities of life, as well as luxuries, we depend on a supply from distances of hundreds and thousands of miles: the whole world contributes in the supply of our food, clothing, building materials, etc.

That means, our existence is dependent on an efficient and reliable system of transportation and distribution of all needs of civilized life. Such has been developed during the last century in the system of steam railroads, which, in taking care of the transportation and distribution of commodities, have made modern civilization possible. For civilization means separation of production, in time and in location, from consumption, to secure maximum economy.

.

The necessities of civilized life consist of two groups. materials and energy Our transportation system takes care of materials, but cannot deal with the supply of energy, and the failure of an efficient energy supply has been and still is the most serious handicap which retards the advance of civilization. The transportation system could deal with the energy supply only in an indirect manner, by the supply of materials as carriers of energy, and when our railroads carry coal it is not the material which we need, but the energy which it carries. But this energy is available only to a very limited extent, as heat, and as mechanical power in big steam units; most of the energy demands of civilized life could not be satisfied by it. In any country village far away from the centers of civilization we have no difficulty to have delivered to us any material produced anywhere in the world; but even in the centers of civilization we could not get the energy to run a sewing machine or drive a fan without *electric power*. Thus, just as our steam railways and express companies take care of the transportation and distribution of materials, so civilization requires a system of transmission and distribution of energy, and our electric circuits are beginning to do this; and just as 50 to 75 years ago in the steam railroads, steamship lines, etc., the system of transportation and distribution of materials was developed, so we see all around us in the electric transmission systems the development of the system of the world's energy transmission in progress of development. When we see local electric distribution systems combining, the big electric systems of our capital cities reaching out over the country, transmission lines interconnecting to· networks covering many thousands of square miles, this is not merely the result of the higher economy of cooperation, of mass production, but it is the same process which took place in the steam railroad world some time ago, as a necessary requirement of coordination to carry out their function as carriers and distributers of materials in the case of the railroads, of energy in the case of the electric systems

We must realize this progress, and the forces which lead to it, so as to understand what is going on, and to assist in the proper development, in avoiding, in the creation of the country's electrical network, whatever mistakes have been made in the development of the country's railway network

Electricity, thus, is taking over the energy supply required by civilization as the only form of energy which, by its simplicity and economy of conversion, combined with economical transmission, is capable of supplying all the energy demands, from the smallest domestic need to the biggest powers. As we now begin to realize, the economic function of the steam engine is not the energy supply at the place of consumption, from the chemical energy of coal—it is too complicated and inefficient for this—but it is the conversion of chemical energy of coal into electrical energy in bulk, for transmission and distribution to the places of consumption.

If, then, electric power takes the place of steam power in our industries, etc., it is not merely the substitution of the electric motor for the steam engine or turbine. Such would rarely realize the best economy. The method of operation in all our industries, and especially those requiring considerable power, is largely—more than usually realized—determined by the characteristics of the power supply, and what is the most economical method with the steam engine as source of power may be very uneconomical with electric power supply, and electric power supply often permits a far more economical method of operation which was impossible with steam power   Thus the introduction of electricity as the medium of distributing the world's energy demand means a reorganization of our industrial methods, to adapt the same to the new form of power

For instance, the steam engine requires skilled attendance, and with its boiler plant, auxiliaries, etc., is a complex apparatus, is economical only in large units.   Thus, when operating a factory or mill by steam power, one large engine is used, driving by shafts and countershafts, by pulleys and belts, and possibly wasting half or more of its energy in the mechanical transmission to the driven machines. But we could not economically place a steam engine at every one of the hundreds of machines in the factory. Substituting electrical power by replacing the engine by one large electric motor would be very uneconomical, as we can place a motor at every driven machine, and these small motors are practically as efficient—within very few per cent —as one big motor would be, and all the belting and shafting, with its waste of energy, inconvenience, and danger, vanishes.   With the steam engine as source of power, to run one or two machines only, to complete some work, requires keeping the big engine in operation, and therefore is extremely wasteful.   With individual electric motors the economy is practically the same, whether only one or two motors are used, or the entire factory is in operation.   On the other hand, with the steam engine, it makes no difference in the cost of power whether it is in operation from 8 a m to 6 p.m , or from 6 a.m. to 4 p.m. With electric power, in the former case the power demand would overlap with whatever lighting load the same supply circuit carries, but would not in the latter case, and the latter case thus would give a better load factor of the electric circuit, and thereby a lower cost of power. Again, with electric power, if very large power demands could be restricted to the periods of light load on the electric supply systems, this would reduce the cost of power. Nothing like this exists with the steam engine.

Electrical energy thus makes the power users economically more dependent upon each other, and thereby exerts a strong force toward industrial coördination—that is, coöperation

Another illustration of the industrial reorganization required to derive the full benefit of electric power is afforded by the traction problem. Very often a study of the electrification of a railway shows no economical advantage in the replacement of the steam locomotive by the electric locomotive, even when considering only passenger service At the same time, an electric railway may parallel the same steam railway, offer better service at lower price, and show financially better returns than the steam railway. But so, also, in the early days of steam, the steam engine in place of the horse in front of the stage coach was no success, and still the stage coach has gone and the steam locomotive has conquered; but it did not by replacing the horse, but by developing a system suited to the characteristics of the steam engine. The same repeats now in the relation of steam traction and electric traction. The steam engine is most economical in the largest units, and the economy of steam railway operation depends on the concentration of the load in as few and as large units as possible therefore, the largest locomotive which can pass through bridges and around curves Exactly the reverse is the condition of economy of electric traction the economy depends on the distribution of the load as uniformly as possible in space and in time—that is, small units at frequent intervals—

and therefore, while steam traction has gone to larger and larger units, in electric traction even the trailer car, so frequently used in the early days, has practically vanished. Obviously, then, the electric motor cannot economically compete with the steam engine under the conditions of maximum economy of steam and minimum economy of electric operation, and electric traction under steam traction conditions shows marked economy only in the case of such heavy service that the maximum permissible train units follow each other at the shortest possible intervals— that is, give maximum uniformity of load—and thus the economic requirements of both forms of power coincide. These two instances may illustrate the changes in industrial operation which the introduction of electric power requires and which are taking place today.

To conclude, then: Electric energy is the only form which is economically suited for general energy transmission and distribution. Civilization depends on the supply of materials and of energy as its two necessities The supply of materials is taken care of by the transportation system of the world. The supply of energy is being developed by the electrical transmission system, which with regard to energy becomes what the railway system is with regard to materials. Introduction of electric power in place of other forms of power rarely can be a mere substitution, but usually requires a change of the methods of power application, a reorganization of the industry, to secure maximum economy.

Before our eyes we thus see today taking place the organization of the universal energy supply of the civilized world, by electric transmission and distribution, and while the details of the structure are still changing and undeveloped, we can already see the general outlines and methods, the general principles of the organization of the generating systems, the transmission and distribution circuits and their interconnection.

The huge metropolitan steam-turbine stations, of hundreds of megawatts capacity, usually are the centers of electric power generation: often several such stations in the same city, as Chicago, New York, etc., tied together into one unit.

Smaller steam-turbine stations at strategic points throughout the country interconnect with the metropolitan system and give control and steadiness to the power.

Where large water powers exist, hydraulic stations feed into the system, and induction generator stations, automatic and without attention, are just beginning to make their appearance in collecting smaller water powers and feeding into the synchronous stations as receivers

In some territories, as Chicago, New York, practically all generation may be by steam turbine, in other hydraulic power may preponderate, as in the South and the far West, or steam and water power may share in the supply, as in the upper Hudson, the Niagara, the New England developments

From the generating stations issue the power distribution lines, supplying power in bulk to substations or to large industries, as railway systems, cities, mills and factories In densely populated districts, as large cities, generating stations as well as power distribution lines usually are about 10,000 volts, the latter underground cable, throughout the country, 33,000 seems to come into favor as the most convenient voltage for power distribution.

Trunk lines then interconnect the generating stations and centers of electrical development, water powers, cities, industrial territories, at voltages of 100 to 200 kilovolts.

On the other side, from the substations supplied by the power distribution circuits, issue for general distribution the primary distribution lines, almost always 2300 volts, or four-wire 2300 volts, that is, 4000 volts between the phases, and from step-down transformers fed by the primary lines then issue the secondary lines, three-wire 110 volts, usually single-phase

We thus see the development of four systems of circuits superimposed upon each other:

The three-wire 110-volt secondary distribution, for lighting and general domestic use, including smaller motors

The 2300-volt primary distribution, single-phase wire for feeding secondary circuits, three-phase for industrial power, etc

The 10,000-volt underground cable or 33,000-volt overhead power distribution, supplying the substations from which radiate the primary distribution circuits, supplying also other distribution substations, as converter substation for 600-volt direct-current railway or three-wire 125-volt direct-current general distribution; supplying also large factories, mills, etc.

The trunk lines of very high voltage, interconnecting the power distribution and generating systems

The power distribution circuits, especially the overhead 33,000-volt ones, less the underground cable systems, frequently are interconnected networks, carrying heavy power. So also are the high-voltage trunk lines networks, of much larger mesh, however, but often carrying less power, rather used to exchange power between systems, with the varying demands of the systems.

Primary and secondary distribution, however, commonly is radial, that is, the feeders are not interconnected, but separately controlled from the stations

As seen, small distributed power and light is supplied from the secondary distribution; larger motors, small factories, etc., from the primary distribution, while large users of powers, as railways, cities and villages, industrial establishments, are served from the power distribution circuits, while the trunk lines serve to unify the entire system

APPENDIX II

OVERHEAD LINE TABLES

Per mile of single wire of three-phase or single-phase line. Solid round copper wire

Size of wire No.	60-cycle reactance, x_{60}, ohms Distance between wires				25-cycle reactance, x_{25}, ohms Distance between wires				Resistance, r, 25°C Ohms	Area, in circular mils Cir. mils	Diameter Mils	Weight Pounds	Size of wire No.
	16 feet	8 feet	4 feet	2 feet	16 feet	8 feet	4 feet	2 feet					
....	0.341	0.382	0.425	0.467	0.145	0.162	0.179	0.196	0.051	1,000,000	1,000	16,000	....
....	0.383	0.425	0.467	0.509	0.162	0.179	0.196	0.213	0.102	500,000	707	8,000	....
....	0.412	0.464	0.506	0.548	0.178	0.195	0.212	0.229	0.204	250,000	500	4,000	....
0000	0.435	0.477	0.519	0.561	0.183	0.200	0.217	0.234	0.260	211,600	460	3,380	0000
000	0.450	0.492	0.534	0.576	0.189	0.206	0.223	0.240	0.330	167,800	410	2,680	000
00	0.462	0.504	0.546	0.588	0.194	0.211	0.228	0.245	0.410	133,080	365	2,125	00
0	0.477	0.519	0.561	0.602	0.200	0.217	0.234	0.251	0.520	105,590	325	1,690	0
1	0.492	0.534	0.576	0.616	0.206	0.223	0.240	0.257	0.650	83,700	289	1,335	1
2	0.504	0.546	0.588	0.630	0.211	0.228	0.245	0.263	0.830	66,370	258	1,060	2
3	0.519	0.561	0.602	0.644	0.217	0.234	0.251	0.269	1.040	52,630	220	840	3
4	0.534	0.576	0.616	0.659	0.223	0.240	0.257	0.275	1.310	41,740	204	670	4
5	0.546	0.588	0.630	0.674	0.228	0.245	0.263	0.281	1.670	33,100	182	530	5
6	0.561	0.602	0.644	0.687	0.234	0.251	0.269	0.287	2.100	26,250	162	420	6
7	0.576	0.616	0.659	0.701	0.240	0.257	0.275	0.292	2.640	20,820	144	335	7
8	0.588	0.630	0.674	0.715	0.245	0.263	0.281	0.298	3.330	16,510	128	265	8
9	0.602	0.644	0.687	0.729	0.251	0.269	0.287	0.304	4.190	13,100	114	210	9
10	0.616	0.659	0.701	0.742	0.257	0.275	0.292	0.309	5.300	10,380	102	166	10

In stranded copper cable the 25-cycle reactance is about 0.007 ohm less, the 60-cycle reactance 0.017 ohm less than in solid round wire of same resistance.

In stranded aluminum cable the 25-cycle reactance is 0.02 ohm less, the 60-cycle reactance about 0.048 ohm less than in solid round copper wire of same resistance.

16